MILLENNIUM PARTY GUIDE

CONTENTS

PARTY IDEAS

GLOBAL PARTY GUIDE

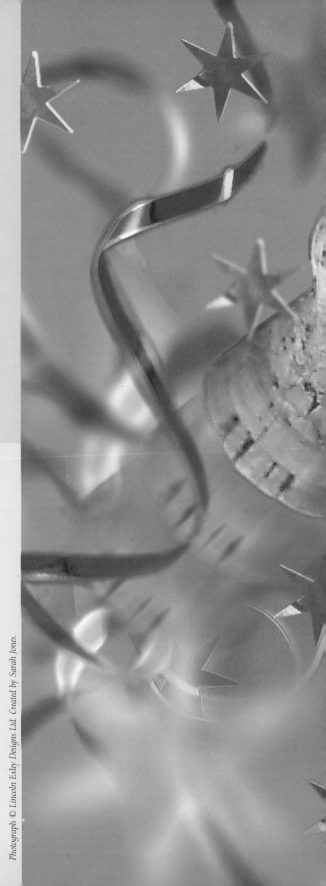

PARTY IDEAS

FOR A MILLENNIUM PARTY TO REMEMBER, CHOOSE A SPECTACULAR LOCATION, OR TRANSFORM A ROOM INTO A STUNNING SETTING. SET UP A FUND FOR A DAZZLING FIREWORK DISPLAY, AND STYLE INVITATIONS AND DECOR TO MATCH YOUR THEME. FINALLY, TAKE TIME OVER FINISHING TOUCHES, SUCH AS LIGHTING, FLOWERS, NAPKINS AND GLASSES.

MM NIGHT

TWO THOUSAND IN ROMAN NUMERALS IS MM, SO ENJOY AN MM NIGHT ON THE EVE OF THE MILLENNIUM. ASK GUESTS TO DRESS AS CHARACTERS, FILMS, ANYTHING BEGINNING WITH THE LETTER "M".

Invite Send out with a request for each guest to donate a firework of a set value, to be delivered before the party.

Costumes Ideas include: Mickey Mouse, Minnie Mouse, Marilyn Monroe, *Mary Poppins*, the Marx Brothers, *The Munsters*, Mighty Mouse, one of the Muppets, *Mad Max* or the millennium bug.

Decor Spray chairs silver, buy silver napkins and tie with silver ribbon, spray fruit silver and attach to name tags.

Food Serve dishes that begin with "M" – try M&M's sweets, marshmallows, meringues and marzipan fruits.

Drinks Moët & Chandon champagne.

Entertainment Erect a huge clock counting down to midnight, then start the firework display.

Photograph © Lincoln Exley Designs Ltd. Created by Sarah Jones.

21ST CENTURY PARTY

INVITE GUESTS TO DRESS IN COSTUMES INSPIRED BY THE 21ST CENTURY AND BY FILMS SUCH AS *WAR OF THE WORLDS*, *INVASION OF THE BODY SNATCHERS*, *CLOSE ENCOUNTERS OF THE THIRD KIND* AND *ALIEN*.

Invite Attach to Polaroids showing a clock with both hands set at midnight.

Costumes Spacemen, martians, astronauts and aliens.

Decor Create a moonscape atmosphere by hiring a dry-ice machine. Cover the windows with reflective silver paper, replace ordinary lightbulbs with blue coloured ones, and hang streamers from every door frame.

Music The soundtrack from *2001: A Space Odyssey*.

Food Keep it simple: huge bowls of chips, dips and canapés to graze on.

Drinks Add a little green food colouring to cocktails.

Entertainment Hand out party poppers, hooters, whistles and bangers to set off at midnight.

DRAGON PARTY

AS THE YEAR 2000 IS THE CHINESE YEAR OF THE DRAGON, CELEBRATE IN ORIENTAL STYLE.

Invite Write on coloured paper fans.

Costumes Wear silk, or dress as a Chinese lion, dragon, or the animal of the Chinese year you were born in. Wear plenty of red, associated with joy and happiness in China.

Decor Hang the walls with kites, fans and paper dragons. Draw Chinese characters on large sheets of white paper, and hang from bamboo canes. Spread the dinner table with sheets of Chinese newspaper and decorate the surrounding area with paper lanterns.

Food Serve Chinese food from rice bowls and bamboo steamers. Eat with chopsticks and wash down the meal with Chinese beer or green tea. Finish the meal with sticky rice cakes, called *lin guo*, and fortune cookies.

Entertainment Let off firecrackers at midnight to scare off evil spirits. Give small gifts in red envelopes to guests.

For a carnival atmosphere,

hang whistles from the ceiling

on long lengths of gold ribbon.

Paint containers of every shape

and size in bright colours,

fill with dried beans and use

as drums and shakers.

CARNIVAL NIGHT EXTRAVAGANZA

THINK RIO, TRINIDAD, EVEN LONDON'S NOTTING HILL, AND RECREATE THE THRILL OF THE SAMBADROME IN BRAZIL, WITH A STEAMY EVENING OF LOUD SAMBA MUSIC, RUM PUNCH AND NON–STOP DANCING.

Invite Attach parcel labels, detailing the venue, time and place, to long, brightly coloured feathers.

Costumes Glamorous high headdresses, feathers and sequins, tiny bikinis (if you dare) for women; ruffled shirts for men.

Decor Decorate tables with African fabric and huge platters of tropical fruit piled into pyramids.

Music Soca and samba – played loud.

Food Easy food that's fun to eat with the fingers: offer rice and peas with fried fish and jerk chicken, plates of skewered vegetables and fish, and sweet potato and plantain crisps. Dice and slice tropical fruit, such as mango, pineapple and papaya, to make a fruit salad, then squeeze over lime juice and lace with white rum.

EXPLORERS & INVENTORS

CELEBRATE THE EXPLORERS AND INVENTORS WHO HAVE HELPED TO SHAPE THE MODERN WORLD, BY USING THEM AS INSPIRATION FOR COSTUME THEMES.

Invite Send on a cut-out photograph of possibly the most useful and oldest invention of all: the wheel.

Costumes Ideas for costumes include: Scott of the Antarctic, David Livingstone, Albert Einstein, Louis Pasteur, Alexander Graham Bell, Archimedes, Jacques Cousteau, Wilbur and Orville Wright, Thomas Alva Edison, Sir Walter Raleigh, Neil Armstrong, Abel Tasman, Marie Curie, Alexander the Great, Captain Cook, Marco Polo, Sir Isaac Newton, the Pharaohs.

Decor Paint a huge mural for the wall featuring inventions such as the telephone, television, clock, camera, bicycle, light bulb, chess set, aeroplane and space rocket.

Entertainment Award a prize at the end of the evening for the most inventive costume.

PARTY VENUES

THE MILLENNIUM IS THE ONE OCCASION FOR WHICH THERE IS NO EXCUSE FOR NOT CELEBRATING TO THE FULL, SO REALLY GO TO TOWN AND HOLD AN ULTIMATE PARTY IN THE ULTIMATE LOCATION:

Paris, Amsterdam or New York ★ Hot-air balloon

Castle ★ Museum ★ Night club

Glacier ★ Boat club ★ Casino

Swimming pool ★ Fiji, Hawaii or Goa

Yacht ★ Ski chalet ★ Chartered, open-topped bus

Cottage in the countryside ★ Beach ★ Art gallery

Barn ★ River boat ★ Vineyard

Cruise liner ★ Waterfall ★ Scuba-diving

Swimming with dolphins ★ Forest ★ Desert

Roof garden restaurant ★ Pier ★ Stately home

Nile cruise boat ★ Wine cellar ★ Fjord

RULERS OF THE MILLENNIUM

FOR A PARTY THAT TRAVELS THROUGH THE AGES, ASK GUESTS TO DRESS AS THE FAMOUS PERSON THEY FEEL SHOULD RULE THE NEXT MILLENNIUM, AND TO BEHAVE AS THAT PERSON FOR THE WHOLE EVENING.

Invite Send out plain paper crowns and invite guests to decorate them in keeping with their chosen ruler and wear them on the night.

Costumes Ask guests to dress as kings and queens, or as powerful figures from history or the present, such as Nebuchadnezzar, Joan of Arc, Genghis Khan, George Washington, Chairman Mao and Nelson Mandela.

Decor Hang opulent drapes made from silk, velvet or brocade on the walls. Embellish the cloth with gold metallic paint, fake gems and gold bobble braiding.

Food Dress staff as attendants or servants, and provide a feast fit for royalty. Cover platters with vine leaves and offer mouthwatering canapés throughout the evening.

SPORTING HEROES PARTY

DRESS AS YOUR FAVOURITE SPORTING HERO OF ALL TIME, AND SPEND AN EVENING DANCING TO RECORDS RATHER THAN BREAKING THEM.

Invite Attach to athletic running numbers.

Costumes Come as football, baseball and athletics stars of today, or as Greek athletes from the first Olympics, Victorian tennis players or golfers from the 1920s.

Decor Paint the five Olympic rings on white sheets and use them as tablecloths. Decorate food with paper flags from around the world, and illuminate the garden with flaming torches.

Music The soundtrack from *Chariots of Fire*.

Entertainment Hold competitive games: a sporting trivia quiz, arm wrestling and team games. Award medals or certificates to the winners.

ECLIPSE PARTY

A FULL ECLIPSE TAKES PLACE IN 1999, HAILING THE COUNTDOWN TO THE MILLENNIUM. CELEBRATE ALL THINGS CELESTIAL WITH A HEAVENLY PARTY.

Invite Written on glittery stars with a silver or gold pen.

Costumes Guests should dress in gold and silver and wear plenty of glitter make-up.

Decor Cut star, sun and moon stencils from card, and spray with silver and gold aerosol paint on to white or dark blue tablecloths. Spray old wooden chairs with gold aerosol paint. Hang up a glitter ball. Attach a net to the ceiling, and fill with gold and silver balloons to be released at midnight.

Music Bill Haley and His Comets, Ziggy Stardust.

Food Gild sweets and cakes with edible loose-leaf gold.

Entertainment Spray disposable cameras silver, and place on tables so guests can capture the evening. Hand out sparklers, and hold a silver and gold firework display.

Illuminate an outdoor party by hanging tiny white fairy lights in trees. Alternatively, paint empty glass jars with translucent glass paint, set with night-lights and suspend with string.

BEACH PARTY

DRESS AS MERMAIDS AND MUSCLE-BOUND SURFERS, AND ENJOY ICE CREAM, FRUIT PUNCH AND CANDYFLOSS. IF YOU CAN'T BE DOWN BY THE SEA, CREATE A BEACH INDOORS.

Costumes Dress in swimming costumes, grass skirts, sea nymph and lifeguard outfits.

Decor Build sandcastles, push flares into the sand and decorate the area with large shells.

Music The Beach Boys, steel drum music.

Entertainment Toasting marshmallows, limbo dancing.

Instead of using glasses

for drinks, offer guests

hollowed-out coconut shells

filled with delicious

tropical cocktails.

TREE-PLANTING PARTY

LEAVE YOUR MARK ON THE PLANET BY JOINING WITH FRIENDS TO PLANT TREES FOR THE FUTURE.

In the run-up to the party, try to get additional funding for trees by contacting local businesses and inviting them to contribute. Ask a local council or wildlife group to designate an area that would benefit from more trees, seeking their advice on planting, too. After planting the trees, invite guests home for a delicious barbecue accompanied by baked potatoes with chilli, soured cream and grated cheese. Reward guests for their hard work by presenting them with bottles of pampering massage oil.

Photograph © Lincoln Exley Designs Ltd. Created by Sarah Jones

2000-GUEST PARTY

USE HEADS OF LOCAL SCHOOLS TO HELP ARRANGE THE BIGGEST PARTY EVER – WITH 2000 PEOPLE AS GUESTS.

Invite Ask each school in your area to the party.

Decor Hold the event in the grounds of the largest school.

Food Ask each school to supply a table of themed food for a certain number of guests. Theme food according to countries or colours.

Music Provided by school orchestras and choirs.

Entertainment Book a professional photographer to photograph all the guests, and give a print to each school.

Organize a party at which you and your friends try to break a world record for the millennium, such as dancing the world's longest conga.

TIME CAPSULE PARTY

INVOLVE EVERY CHILD IN THE FAMILY, OR EVEN IN THE STREET, ASKING THEM TO HELP FILL A TIME CAPSULE FOR THE NEXT MILLENNIUM.

Invite each child to fill a blank page with a poem or story about their lives or about the millennium. Include a snap-shot of each child and their signature, and bind the loose pages into an album. Other suitable items for the capsule include: national and local newspapers, fashion magazines, a payslip, a car brochure and newly minted coins. Video the album being made and the capsule being filled, and enclose in the capsule.

For striking party glasses, paint swirls of gold relief paint on plain wine glasses.

FANCY-DRESS THEMES

Dracula ★ *Superheroes* ★ *Cleopatra*
Mulan ★ *The Spice Girls* ★ Zorro
Star Trek ★ *Football legends* ★ Titanic
Fairy tales ★ *Hollywood stars*
X Files ★ *Pirates* ★ Guys and Dolls
On safari ★ Strictly Ballroom
Outlaws ★ *Carmen Miranda*
Night of Eastern Promise ★ Oklahoma
The circus ★ Evita ★ Star Wars
Abba ★ *Knights and maidens*
The Great Gatsby ★ *Back to school*

MASQUERADE PARTY

SEND OUT INVITATIONS ASKING GUESTS TO WEAR SPECTACULAR MASKS.

Allow guests to choose any shape of mask and to let their imagination run riot in embellishing the masks with paint, feathers and sequins. Guests should wear the masks until midnight, when they reveal their true identities. Award a bottle of champagne for the best creation.

STREET PARTY

CLUB TOGETHER WITH NEIGHBOURS TO THROW A HUGE STREET PARTY.

Arrange to have the road cordoned off for the evening, then line the street with trestle tables laden with delicious food. Book magicians, stilt-walkers and fire eaters to entertain guests, then encourage everyone to join in a torch-lit procession at midnight.

MOGHUL BANQUET

ENJOY AN EVENING EATING DELICIOUS SPICY FOOD IN SUMPTUOUS SURROUNDINGS.

Deck a marquee with silk screens and drape brilliantly coloured silk or muslin around the walls and ceiling to create a canopy effect. Scent the venue with jasmine incense sticks, and light the room with small night-lights. After a magnificent banquet, sound in the new year with drums and tiny bells.

Add glitz to party napkins by sewing on a shimmering ribbon trim.

MILLENNIUM MURAL

PAINT A HUGE MURAL to celebrate the millennium. First obtain permission and funding from your local authority. Invite a local artist to draw a design for the side of a local building such as a sports hall, theatre, cinema or shopping centre. Divide the mural into sections and invite local nurseries, schools, colleges and charity groups to complete a section each. Hold a party at the mural's official unveiling, to thank everyone for their help.

TANGO PARTY

THROW A PARTY WHERE PASSION, GRACE AND VERVE REIGN SUPREME, IN A NIGHT DEDICATED TO DANCING THE TANGO.

Invite guests to dress in slinky evening wear, and decorate the venue to resemble an elegant dance hall of the 1920s. Hire a dance teacher for the night, to teach guests the art of dancing the tango, and then dance until dawn.

FINAL TOUCHES

STYLE DECOR TO MAKE A
STUNNING BACKDROP
FOR THE ULTIMATE NEW
YEAR'S EVE PARTY.

PERSONALIZED WINE BOTTLES

GIVE A PARTY GIFT to remember: print striking personalized wine labels celebrating the millennium. Include guests' names, the date and the party location. Steam off labels from bottles of good red wine and replace them with your own labels. Guests can then lay the wine down for the future.

MILLENNIUM PLATES

IMMORTALIZE YOUR PARTY by painting crockery to record the event. Use thermohardening water-based ceramic paint on inexpensive white china plates to paint each guest's name, the date of the party and, if you are artistic, a picture of the venue or the guest. Use the plates during supper, then offer the clean plates as gifts when guests leave.

TEQUILA TOAST

FOR THE ULTIMATE in stylish extravagance, add loose-leaf gold to tequila. Peel two sheets of 24-carat gold leaf from the backing paper and put in a blender with a small amount of clear tequila. Blend for 20 seconds, then add enough ice-cold tequila to serve the number of guests present. Pour into small shot glasses and toast the new millennium in style.

GILDED LEAF NAPKINS

GLAMOROUS GILDED LEAVES are ideal for adorning napkins. Flatten pretty leaves between sheets of blotting paper in the pages of a heavy book. When dry, attach a short length of wire to each stalk, and lightly spray the leaves with gold aerosol paint. Spray gold a wooden curtain ring for each guest and, using the wire, attach three leaves to each ring. Bind the ring with gold ribbon to hide the wire, and slip in a rolled linen napkin.

Spell guests' names out with red and green jelly beans, and use as festive place settings.

LUSTROUS PLACE SETTING

THESE WONDERFUL PLACE SETTINGS shine brilliantly on a party table. Write each guest's name on a small terracotta pot using a glue gun or masking fluid. Spray the pot with gold aerosol paint and leave to dry. Peel off the glue or masking fluid to reveal the guest's name written in terracotta. Plant with small blooms and sit a pot on each dinner plate.

PARTY DECOR TIPS

★ CREATE YOUR OWN dazzling millennium tablecloth for the evening by transforming velvet cloth with gold metallic paint and ornate tassels.

★ ADD A BOLD, BRIGHT TOUCH to napkins: tie them with an attractive wide ribbon, then tuck a tulip or gerbera flower under each ribbon.

★ GARNISH COCKTAILS with stylish lemon spirals, strawberry fans, melon balls and cherries on stems.

GOLDEN PEAR PLACE SETTINGS

GILD A CELEBRATORY TABLE with glittering pear place settings. Wash fresh pears in soapy water and dry them well. Spray the pears with gold aerosol paint. When dry, push a small silk leaf into the top of each pear and tie on a hand-written parcel label with the guest's name.

GLOBAL PARTY GUIDE

THERE ARE FEW BETTER EXCUSES FOR A PARTY THAN TO WELCOME A NEW MILLENNIUM. COUNTRIES ACROSS THE WORLD WILL PARTY IN THEIR OWN STYLE AND AT THEIR OWN TIME. HOWEVER, ALL WILL BE UNITED IN WHAT PROMISES TO BE THE BIGGEST GLOBAL CELEBRATION IN HISTORY.

TONGA

★ **Tonga's** claim to be the first nation to see in the millennium has been questioned by the nearby Republic of Kiribati. Despite this, the island nation has great plans to celebrate, including a month-long millennium festival culminating in New Year's Day celebrations. The festival has both sporting and musical themes, and will include fishing and golfing competitions, brass bands and native cultural exhibitions. Web: http://www.tonga2000.net/

FIJI

★ **Fiji** is west of the International Date Line, but just misses out as the first nation to greet the dawn of the new millennium. Nevertheless, it is making much of the fact that the 180° meridian passes through the main island, Viti Levu. This is the venue of the main New Year's Eve festivity, the "Dusk 'Til Dawn" concert. Web: http://www.bulafiji.com/2000.htm

NEW ZEALAND

★ **Gisborne**, on the eastern tip of the North Island, holds an annual First Light Festival, and claims to be the first city to see the sun of the new millennium. A larger than ever New Year's Eve festival is promised for 1999, with the Millennium and Town Clocks the focus of live entertainment through the night. Tel: (64) 04 495 7266.

★ **The Pacific Tall Ships Festival** reaches New Zealand in December 1999, and targets Gisborne in time to see in the new millennium, with some ships sailing to the international date line 160 km (100 miles) to the east. Web: http://www.enternet.co.nz/client/personal/steve/

★ **Te Mata Peak**, just outside the town of Hastings, is believed to be the first point in New Zealand to catch the rays of the dawn of the new millennium. As such, a huge party is planned for New Year's Eve 1999, with dawn celebrations the morning after. Web: http://www.hawkesbay.com/millenn.html

AUSTRALIA

ALTHOUGH PEOPLE IN AUSTRALIA WILL BE FOCUSING ON THE OLYMPIC GAMES BEING HELD IN SYDNEY IN 2000, EACH MAJOR CITY PLANS SPECTACULAR CELEBRATIONS FOR THE MILLENNIUM.

★ **Sydney Harbour** will be the backdrop of one of Australia's biggest millennium celebrations. A huge fireworks display is planned to set the harbour alight, and up to two million people are expected to enjoy a variety of live entertainment and cultural activities.

★ **Sydney Opera House** is the stunning venue for a New Year's Eve mask party, organized by the Millennial Foundation along with 30 other parties worldwide, and hosted by the Mayor of Sydney. Guests will have the best possible view of the huge fireworks display in the harbour. Web: http://www.yes2000.co.uk

★ **The Melbourne Millennium Committee** is organizing a community-based New Year's Eve party in 1999, featuring fireworks displays and street parties positioned in various venues at the centre of the city.

★ **Cape Byron**, the easternmost tip of Australia, will be the first place in the country to greet the new millennium. As such, big celebrations are planned to see in the new year.

ISRAEL

★ **The Holy Land** will be a major focus of celebration and pilgrimage, with over four million visitors expected to converge on Israel and Palestine at the turn of the millennium. Numerous special events to commemorate the 2000th anniversary of the birth of Christ are planned, in particular in Jerusalem, Nazareth and Bethlehem. Tel: (972) 22 741 323 or (972) 22 742 224.

EGYPT

★ **Cheop's pyramid**, Giza, will have a 2.75m (9ft) golden cover set on it from dusk of 31 December 1999 to the dawn of the new millennium. There will also be a 12-hour light show directed by Jean-Michel Jarre. Tel: (20) 02 391 3454.

SOUTH AFRICA

★ **In Cape Town**, in December 1999, the Council for the Parliament of the World's Religions will convene. The Parliament is asking groups, nations and religious communities to donate strategic millennium gifts that will benefit "our planetary community". Tel: (1) 312 629 2990.

★ **Table Mountain**, above Cape Town, is the imposing venue for a New Year's Eve "Trance" party planned for New Year's Eve 1999, featuring leading psychedelic trance bands, with the aim of blending nature with technology. Web: http://www.southafrica2000.com

UNITED KINGDOM

ENGLAND

THE ARRIVAL OF THE MILLENNIUM WILL BE MARKED BY A NATIONWIDE PEALING OF CHURCH BELLS. OVER 400 CHURCHES WILL ALSO HAVE NEWLY INSTALLED FLOODLIGHTS SWITCHED ON.

★ **Greenwich, London**, is the historical location of the Prime Meridian, which dictates the time zones of the world and is the focus of British millennium celebrations with The Millennium Experience. On New Year's Eve 1999, the opening ceremony of the huge Millennium Dome on the Greenwich Peninsula will herald a gala night for 35,000 people, including the Queen, the Prince of Wales and the Prime Minister, as well as members of the public. Tel: (44) 0171 808 8200; Web: http://www.dome2000.co.uk

★ **Greenwich Meridian 2000** centres on a New Year's Eve party in Greenwich Park for 50,000 people, featuring a huge musical spectacular. A 24-hour global telecast on giant screens will show parties as they happen around the world. Tel: (44) 0181 312 6745.

★ **Trafalgar Square** is a traditional London venue to celebrate New Year's Eve, and a record number of revellers are expected to gather to see in the new millennium.

★ **The South Bank of the Thames**, opposite Westminster, is the location for the British Airways London Eye, the biggest Ferris wheel ever to be built. It will be 135m (450ft) high, and will take 30 minutes to complete one full rotation. Tel: (44) 0171 229 9907.

★ **Newcastle's** millennium celebrations on New Year's Eve 1999, will feature a huge sound and light spectacular, involving local artists and highlighting the city's rich cultural heritage. A grand parade featuring lanterns of hope will travel through the city centre to the quayside and along the river, where music, fireworks and laser shows will greet the new millennium. Tel: (44) 0191 261 0610.

SCOTLAND

★ **Hogmanay in Edinburgh** has become one of the largest outdoor events in Europe, attracting crowds of over 350,000. The millennium party is guaranteed to be the biggest yet. Tel: (44) 0131 473 1999.

★ **Glasgow's Hogmanay celebrations**, held annually, are inevitably overshadowed by the scenes in Edinburgh. Nevertheless, the organizers of the 1999 celebrations are determined to put on an event to rival their compatriots'. Tel: (44) 0990 992 244.

★ **The Millennia airship**, launched by Virgin from Edinburgh on New Year's Eve 1999, will attempt a record-breaking world tour, stopping at Greenwich, Paris, Moscow, Hong Kong and finally Sydney, in time for the 2000 Olympics. Web: http://www.edinburghshogmanay.org

WALES

★ **Cardiff's 75,000–seater Millennium Stadium**, with retractable roof, is the venue for the Rugby World Cup Final in September 1999. The huge New Year's Eve party planned to be held in the arena after the tournament promises to be the biggest millennium celebration in Wales. Tel: (44) 01222 232 661.

★ **Cardiff's "Calennig"** will be a community-based millennium celebration, featuring fireworks displays, light shows, funfair rides and musical stages, set around four of the city's main landmarks. Tel: (44) 01222 227 281.

NORTHERN IRELAND

★ **The Strangford Stone** is a huge granite monolith, to be erected in Delamont County Park, Killyleagh, in June 1999. It will be a monument to the teamwork of the divided communities who have united to plan it together.

IRELAND

★ **In Dublin**, "Mile Atha Cliath Teoranta" has been formed with the assistance of Dublin Corporation. It is headed by the Lord Mayor of Dublin, and acts as a focal point for projects to mark the millennium. Web: http://www.dublin-2000.com/

FRANCE

DESPITE THE FEARS OF A POSSIBLE CHAMPAGNE SHORTAGE, THERE SHOULD BE PLENTY OF NON-VINTAGE BUBBLY AVAILABLE: CURRENT STOCKS STAND AT 1 BILLION BOTTLES.

★ **The Eiffel Tower**, standing in the Parc du Champ de Mars, Paris, is the venue for France's biggest millennium party. After the scheduled sound and light spectacular, the Tower will lay a giant luminous "egg", which will crack open to show images of millennium parties around the world. The Tower will also be fitted with over 1000 spotlights to bathe the area in light as the dawn of the new millennium arrives. Tel: (33) 01 49 525 354.

★ **The Tour de la Terre** (Earth Tower) in central Paris will be 650 feet high with a 3000 square-metre platform housing bars, restaurants and exhibition areas, with the environment being a central theme. The tower will form an impressive landmark, and aims to emulate the Eiffel Tower by representing France's modernity.

★ **The River Seine** will be filled with 2000 brightly coloured plastic fish visible from the banks. There are also plans to perfume the Seine for the millennium.

★ **The Pompidou Centre**, the Grand Palais and the Louvre, three great Parisian centres of culture, are all undergoing major upgrades for Paris's 2000 celebration.

★ **The Millennium Countdown Clock** will be centred on the Place Charles de Gaulle, Paris, where twelve avenues, marking the points on the clock face, converge. A powerful laser will form the second hand, sweeping around from the top of the Arc de Triomphe.

★ **The Boulevard Périphérique**, Paris's ring road, will become a vast concert venue for many types of bands and musical events on New Year's Eve 1999.

★ **Marseille** is the starting point for La Course, a round-the-world boat race, which sails on 31 December 2000.

GERMANY

★ **Berlin** is competing with the rest of the world to host the biggest party to mark the beginning of the new millennium. A major spectacle is planned for the city centre on New Year's Eve 1999, centring on an hour-long fireworks display at the Brandenburg Gate, which will also be the venue for bands and theatrical performances.

★ **Düsseldorf Fair** will be the venue for one of Europe's biggest, and possibly longest, millennium celebrations. In addition to the fairground rides and attractions, a variety of live music and entertainment will be on offer. The party is scheduled to start on New Year's Eve 1999, and will continue through the next two days, making what the organizers hope will be the longest New Year's Eve Party ever. Tel: (49) 211 9523 2000.

★ **Oberammergau** will host over 100 performances of the famous Passion Play, commemorating the life of Christ, from May to September 2000. Tel: (49) 08822 92310.

ITALY

★ **Rome** is bracing itself for a record number of visitors for the Great Jubilee. From Christmas 1999 to January 2000, over 13 million tourists and pilgrims are expected to visit the city and its basilicas to celebrate the 2000th anniversary of the incarnation of Christ and the start of the third millennium of Christianity. Tel: (39) 06 49711; Web: http://www.roma2000.it/

★ **Bologna** has been designated one of nine European Cities of Culture, and exhibitions and festivals are being held throughout the year. Tel: (39) 051 204 606.

NETHERLANDS

★ **Den Helder's Fort Kijkduin** hosts the Netherlands's largest New Year's Eve celebration, featuring live musical acts, various entertainment and themed bars in its labyrinth of tunnels. Tel: (31) 223 642 305; Web: http://www.trefnet.nl/kvnh/entree-2000

BELGIUM

★ **Brussels** is one of the nine European Cities of Culture that are co-ordinating their programmes to create "a European cultural space for the year 2000". Brussels 2000 is organizing a large range of activities throughout the year, with a focus on the visual arts, theatre and dance. Tel: (32) 02 214 2000.

SPAIN

★ **Madrid's** Puerto del Sol is the traditional venue for a New Year's Eve party, and the millennium celebrations in 1999 promise to be the biggest ever. The thousands of people who are expected to turn up to hear Spain's most famous clock strike midnight will first enjoy a spectacular fireworks display and musical extravaganza. Tel: (34) 91 429 4951.

★ **Santiago de Compostela** has good reasons to celebrate the new millennium: 1999 marks the jubilee of St. James, its Patron Saint, while it has been designated one of nine European Cities of Culture in 2000. The town has wide-ranging celebration plans, including festivals, art exhibitions and building programmes. Tel: (34) 981 584 081; Web: compostela2000@corevia.com

SWITZERLAND

★ **Geneva's** New Year's Eve celebrations, organized by Signe 2000 on 31 December 1999, will be based on the theme of the four elements: fire, water, air and earth. Web: http://www.swisstin.com/

AUSTRIA

★ **Vienna's Hofburg Palace**, the venue for The Imperial Ball on New Year's Eve 1999, offers one of the most sophisticated Millennium Eve parties in Europe. A gala banquet is followed by dancing in the magnificent state apartments, with bands and orchestras set to take guests into the New Year. Tel: (43) 587 366 623.

★ **The New Year's Trail** in downtown Vienna features a mile-long stretch of festivities ranging through the city centre. The Millennium Eve celebrations promise to be the best ever, with bands, dancers and street entertainers.

POLAND

★ **The Kraków 2000 Festival** builds upon the city's status as one of nine European Cities of Culture, and its increasing popularity as a short-break destination. The theme for the festival, "Spirituality – The Faces of God", featuring various theatrical and musical events, reflects the city's traditional religious diversity. Tel: (48) 12 422 6091.

NORWAY

★ **Bergen 2000** aims to be Norway's largest cultural celebration, with exhibitions, shows and entertainments centred around the new Frescohall, Norway's biggest ever information centre. The theme of the celebrations will be "Art, Work, and Leisure". Tel: (47) 5555 2000.

★ **Oslo** enjoys a double celebration at the turn of the millennium, with the arrival of its 1000-year jubilee. There are plans for a massive fireworks party in the city centre.

FINLAND

★ **Helsinki Arena 2000** plans to celebrate with a virtual Helsinki in cyberspace. The project has widespread national support, and plans will culminate in the year 2000 with a completed three-dimensional model of the city. Web: http://www.helsinkiarena2000.fi/

ICELAND

★ **Reykjavik** is a European City of Culture in the year 2000, and promises a non-stop programme of festivities. Among these are the Reykjavik Millennium Art Festival, the Millennial Celebration of Christianity and the Millennial Celebration of the Discovery of America from Iceland. Tel: (354) 575 2000; Web: http://www.reykjavik2000.is

UNITED STATES

THERE ARE CURRENTLY BIG PLANS FOR NEW YEAR'S EVE MILLENNIUM PARTIES IN ALL THE MAJOR US CITIES. EACH WILL BE TRYING TO MATCH THE TRADITIONAL CELEBRATIONS IN NEW YORK'S TIMES SQUARE.

NEW YORK CITY

★ **Times Square 2000** is set to attract over one million people on New Year's Eve 1999, with a similar celebration expected a year later. The 24-hour celebration will salute the coming of the new millennium by linking each of the world's time zones through giant TV screens. It will start at 7.00am (EST), when the new year first arrives in the Pacific Islands, and will then broadcast live scenes from each of the world's 24 time zones. Tel: (212) 768 1560; Web: http://www.igc.apc.org/millennium/events/mega.html

BOSTON

★ **The First Night group**, based in Boston, promotes alcohol-free celebrations on New Year's Eve, supported by 170 communities across the US and Canada. Parties are usually community-based and include street parades and entertainment, music, theatre and fireworks displays. Tel: (212) 617 542 1399; Web: http://www.firstnight.org/

WASHINGTON DC

★ **The White House Millennium Programme** will highlight projects that recognize the creativity of the American people. Projects include funding for the arts, culture, scientific exploration, technological discovery, education and preserving the environment. Web: http://www.whitehouse.gov/initiatives/millennium/index.shtml

MIAMI

★ **New Year on South Beach** is promoting itself as the New Year's Eve warm alternative to New York. There will be a huge party with fireworks, and music and video towers along the beach. Web: http://southbeach.org

NEW ORLEANS

★ **Jackson Square**, at the heart of New Orleans' French Quarter, will be packed full of revellers seeing in the millennium. The traditional combination of jazz musicians, artists and street performers, as well as a huge fireworks display, will keep the crowds entertained.

CALIFORNIA

★ **Exposition 2000**, a three-day event beginning at sunset, 31 December 1999, is expected to attract over 250,000 people to San Diego's Balboa Park. The park is to be transformed into a cultural extravaganza, with a mix of music, fireworks, entertainment stages, hospitality tents and craft activities, with local museums participating.

★ **The Mojave Desert** witnesses a two-day spiritual event from New Year's Eve 1999. Organizers hope to create the world's largest drumming and chanting circle. Web: http://www.WhisperedPrayers.com/

★ **Party 2000** is to take place on 4000 acres of land between Palm Springs and the Arizona border. Organizers claim they will host the largest fireworks display ever held. The party will last for three days, with live entertainment on five stages, and should feature many big-name bands. Web: http//www.party2000.com/

CANADA

★ **Cape Spear** in Newfoundland is the easternmost point on the North American continent, and will be the first place in North America to see the dawn of the new millennium. A "First Light" party is being organized at the point, to welcome the millennium's dawn.

★ **Toronto 2000 – An Urban Odyssey** will consist of a series of celebrations and a New Year's Eve gala on 31 December 1999. Tel: (416) 292 0206; Web: http://www.torontomillennium.com/

★ **Halifax, Nova Scotia** also celebrates its 250th birthday on New Year's Eve 1999. Organizers are planning a variety of cultural events and entertainment. Tel: (902) 420 4724.

★ **The Montreal International Jazz Festival** will feature a huge millennium party on New Year's Eve 1999, with a series of performances promised by some of the jazz world's biggest stars, on outdoor stages and in indoor clubs. Tel: (514) 523 3378.

★ **In Vancouver**, the ongoing MV 2000! event culminates in New Year's Eve celebrations in 1999. All-night parties are planned, along with a time-capsule project, a Futurist's Festival and a Festival of Time. Tel: (604) 618 5825.

COSTA RICA

★ **Costa Rica's** six-day millennium celebration, starting on 27 December 1999, promises to be a high-profile affair, with the United Nations peace conference as its centrepiece. Many of the world's leading politicians and environmentalists will be present, and celebrations will feature a giant fireworks display and a series of live bands.

BRAZIL

★ **Rio de Janeiro's Copacabana Beach** is the glamorous setting for one of the world's biggest free parties, with over 2.5 million revellers expected to attend. The countdown to the new millennium will feature a bigger-than-ever carnival on the eight-mile stretch of beach, with a variety of live bands and a huge fireworks display.

SAMOA

★ **The 20th century** and the current millennium finally come to a close in Samoa, the nation closest to the International Date Line on its eastern side. Celebrations, thanksgivings and blessings will be centred in the capital, Apia, on the island of Upolu. The ultimate millennium countdown will culminate in a nationwide pealing of church bells at the stroke of midnight, and a huge fireworks display and festival. Web: http://www.samoa.co.uk

THE
MILLENNIUM
PARTY BOOK

THE
MILLENNIUM
PARTY BOOK

PARTY IDEAS
LAUREN FLOODGATE

FOOD & DRINK
LUCY KNOX & SARAH LOMAN

PARTY PLANNING
SARAH LEVENS

PHOTOGRAPHY
SIMON SMITH

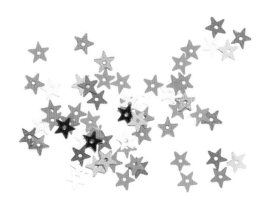

DORLING KINDERSLEY LTD
London • New York • Sydney • Moscow
www.dk.com

A Dorling Kindersley Book

Project Editor Monica Chakraverty
Editor David Summers
Art Editor Lisa Goldsworthy
DTP Designer Bridget Roseberry
Senior Art Editor Tracey Ward
Managing Editor Susannah Marriott
Deputy Art Director Carole Ash
Production Controller Martin Croshaw
Stylist Clare Louise Hunt

First published in Great Britain in 1999
by Dorling Kindersley Limited
9 Henrietta Street, London WC2E 8PS

Copyright © 1999 Dorling Kindersley Limited

www.dk.com

*This book is dedicated to my mum,
for all we've been through together.*

A CIP catalogue record for this book is available from
the British Library

ISBN 0 7513 0700 9

Reproduced in Singapore by Colourscan
Printed and bound in Italy by LEGO

CONTENTS

INTRODUCTION

I HAVE ALWAYS LOVED PARTIES AND CAN STILL REMEMBER THE THRILL AND EXCITEMENT OF GOING TO MY FIRST PROPER PARTY AS A LITTLE GIRL AGED FIVE. MY ENTHUSIASM WAS HARD TO CONTAIN; DRESSED UP IN A LONG FROCK, MY HAIR IN PLAITS AND RIBBONS, I SPENT THE AFTERNOON PLAYING GAMES, EATING CRISPS AND CAKE, AND GUZZLING FIZZY DRINKS.

TODAY, I PREFER TO DRINK A LARGE GIN AND TONIC OR A GLASS OF CHAMPAGNE, AND THE FOOD I SERVE AT PARTIES RANGES FROM SAUSAGES AND MASH TO SOPHISTICATED CANAPÉS, WHILE THE PARTY GAMES ARE OF THE AFTER-DINNER VARIETY. BUT HOWEVER MUCH THE DETAILS HAVE CHANGED, THE ESSENCE, AND MY SHEER ENJOYMENT OF A GOOD PARTY, REMAIN THE SAME.

WHATEVER THE OCCASION OR TYPE OF PARTY – A LARGE-SCALE BALL FOR A WEDDING, A FORMAL BIRTHDAY DINNER, AN INFORMAL BARBECUE WITH FRIENDS OR A SPUR-OF-THE-MOMENT PICNIC ON THE BEACH – THE KEY TO A SUCCESSFUL CELEBRATION

IS THAT FRIENDS AND FAMILY ENJOY THEMSELVES. I HOPE THIS BOOK WILL HELP YOU ACHIEVE JUST THAT, AND CREATE A DAY TO REMEMBER. YOU CAN PLAN A WHOLE PARTY FOLLOWING THE IDEAS FOR INVITATIONS, MENU SUGGESTIONS AND GAMES, OR JUST TAKE ONE IDEA OR THEME AND ADAPT IT TO YOUR TASTE.

WHEN I WAS ASKED TO WRITE THIS BOOK, THE CHALLENGE WAS TO COME UP WITH PARTY SUGGESTIONS THAT WERE PRACTICAL, AFFORDABLE AND WORKABLE WHILE STILL BEING FUN AND ORIGINAL. THE IDEAS FEATURED CATER FOR ALL AGES AND EVERY OCCASION. I HOPE YOU WILL HAVE AS MUCH FUN PLANNING AND ENJOYING YOUR PARTIES AS I HAVE HAD WRITING THIS BOOK.

Lauren Floodgate

CELEBRATE IN STYLE WITH A COCKTAIL PARTY, WHETHER YOU ARE PLANNING AN INFORMAL SOIRÉE OR HOSTING A FORMAL DRINKS PARTY. BE IMAGINATIVE – CHOOSE A THEME SUCH AS GLAMOROUS HOLLYWOOD GLITZ OR A TITANIC-STYLE NAUTICAL NIGHT, SELECT DRINKS AND FOOD TO MATCH, AND SUGGEST

COCKTAIL PARTIES

GUESTS DRESS TO SUIT THE OCCASION. COCKTAILS SERVED FROM THE RIGHT GLASS SEEM TO IMPROVE IN TASTE. DRINK CHAMPAGNE COCKTAILS IN TALL FLUTES, MARTINIS AND MARGARITAS IN TRIANGULAR GLASSES AND PUNCHES AND DAIQUIRIS IN ROUNDED GOBLETS. GARNISH COCKTAILS WITH CITRUS FRUITS AND STAR FRUIT AND WITH EDIBLE FLOWER- OR FRUIT-FILLED ICE CUBES.

SPAGHETTI WESTERN ▷

AN EVENING OF BANDITS, OUTLAWS AND NE'ER-DO-WELLS. CREATE A SALOON SETTING, OR, IF HOLDING THIS PARTY OUTDOORS, BUILD A CAMPFIRE.

Invite Take a picture of yourself wearing a false moustache and sombrero and use it to make up a "wanted" poster, inviting your guests to come in disguise.

Costumes Ponchos and sombreros, cowboy boots and spurs, big moustaches and three-day stubble.

Music The Gipsy Kings, the soundtrack to *The Good, The Bad and The Ugly*, mariachi music, or a little latin rumba.

Table Paint terracotta pots with emulsion paint, and plant up with baby cacti (*see right*). Use a bright tablecloth.

Food Bandits love a feast, so cook up spicy chorizo sausage and meatballs with red sauce (*see page 93*). Serve with refried beans, nachos, tacos and red hot salsa.

Drinks Start with Tequila Sunrise (*see below*). Later, serve margaritas (*see page 90*) or "slam" tequila (*see below*). Arriba!

DRINKS FOR BANDITS

Tequila Sunrise Pour 30ml (1fl oz) tequila into a tall glass filled with crushed ice. Top with orange juice, and drizzle grenadine syrup into the centre of the drink.

Tequila Slammer Pour 30ml (1fl oz) tequila into a tall glass and top up with lemonade. Place your hand over the glass, bang it carefully on the table, and drink.

SEA-FARING COCKTAILS

Sea Waves Pour 45ml (1½fl oz) vodka and 15ml (½fl oz) each of dry vermouth, Blue Curaçao and Galliano over ice.

Blue Lagoon Pour 45ml (1½fl oz) each of Blue Curaçao and vodka over ice. Top up with lemon-lime soda.

Sex on the Beach Stir 30ml (1fl oz) each of vodka and peach schnapps and 60ml (2fl oz) each of orange and cranberry juice into a tall glass half-filled with ice.

Green Bubbles Pour 30ml (1fl oz) each of poire william and Midori into a glass. Top up with chilled champagne.

WHAT WERE YOU DOING WHEN THE SHIP WENT DOWN?

INVITE GUESTS TO SPEND A NIGHT ON THE OCEAN WAVES, PLAYING QUOITS AND CROQUET, GAMBLING IN YOUR HOME-MADE CASINO, OR PLAYING CARDS. FINISH THE EVENING SINGING SEA SHANTIES BY MOONLIGHT.

Decor Set plenty of hurricane lamps around the room and cover surfaces with pebbles and sea shells. Deck walls with lobster pots and fishermen's nets.

Music Play a soundtrack of whale, dolphin or seagull cries, or a record of accordion music.

Food On the captain's table, serve a seafood buffet of oysters, prawns, lobster and crab on an ice tray (*see page 78*).

Drinks Welcome your passengers with Aquavit, Sea Waves, Blue Lagoon, Sex on the Beach or Green Bubbles cocktails (*see left*). Finish the evening with hot buttered rum: heat 60ml (2fl oz) rum, 75ml (2½fl oz) water and 1tsp sugar in a pan. Add a small cinnamon stick, 4 drops of vanilla essence, 1 pinch of nutmeg and 1tsp butter. Serve when the butter melts.

JAMES BOND ▽

SERVE BLINI WITH QUAIL'S EGGS AND SMOKED FISH (SEE PAGE 89). THEN TOAST THE QUEEN WITH VODKA MARTINI (SHAKEN NOT STIRRED), OR WITH A GLASS OF CHAMPAGNE.

Invite Set the scene by sending each guest a toy water pistol attached to a parcel label (*see below*).

Costumes As every Bond fan knows, he is nothing if not impeccably dressed. As an alternative to wearing black ties and Saville Row suits, guests could dress as their favourite character, maybe as a Bond Girl scantily clad in a bikini, or as Odd Job, Jaws, Q, M, Moneypenny, Dr. No or Drax.

Decor Place a hatstand by the front door for bowler hats; hang Union Jacks on the walls.

Music Play anything by John Barrie or a compilation soundtrack of the Bond films.

Table Serve the meal using your best china, glasses and silverware. After dinner, cover the dining table with green baize, and set up a toy roulette wheel, inviting guests to gamble with piles of chocolate money pennies.

To make a martini, shake together 90ml (3fl oz) gin, 30ml (1fl oz) dry vermouth and crushed ice. Strain into a martini glass and add an olive.

1950s HOLLYWOOD

FOR AN EVENING OF GLITZ, ASK GUESTS TO DRESS AS MOVIE STARS FROM THIS GLAMOROUS ERA.

Invite Send out invitations attached to photographs of Hollywood stars of the 1950s, or to pictures of old cars, such as Buicks and T-birds.

Costumes Invite guests to don their slingbacks, dig out their seamed stockings, apply some lipstick and go for glamour. Guests should dress as favourite movie stars of the era, such as Marilyn Monroe, Grace Kelly, Clark Gable and Cary Grant.

Decor Project old cine film on to the wall, and put up Hitchcock film posters.

Music Ask guests to bring along some of their favourite vinyl records. Find an old gramophone and let the music of Elvis Presley, Buddy Holly and Jerry Lee Lewis set the tone for an evening of nostalgia.

Drinks Pink gins (*see page 91*), champagne and rum punch.

COCKTAIL FOOD

SALMON PINWHEELS
(SEE PAGE 86)

CARAMELIZED ONION QUICHES
(SEE PAGE 86)

PUFF PASTRY PIZZAS
(SEE PAGE 88)

CHEESE TWISTS (SEE PAGE 88)

HERBY GARLIC MIXED OLIVES
(SEE PAGE 89)

BALLROOM DANCING

THIS IS A GREAT PARTY FOR A LARGE GROUP OF PEOPLE WHO DO NOT KNOW EACH OTHER.

Send invitations attached to large paper numbers that guests can pin to their clothes. Send matching numbers to different guests, who must introduce themselves at the party to the person wearing the same number and ask them for the first dance. Dance the rumba, salsa, waltz and bossa nova.

COCKTAIL PARTY TIPS

★ Try some more unusual cocktail garnishes: cut lily flower shapes out of kumquats; tie citrus bows from thin slices of peel; twist slices of fruit, then thread securely on to cocktail sticks.

★ Make sure your corkscrew is not waylaid: tie it to elastic and secure it to the door of the refrigerator.

★ To keep drinks cool, bury bottles in a bath or clean dustbin part-filled with ice.

COME AS A COCKTAIL

THROW A COCKTAIL PARTY, INVITING GUESTS TO DRESS UP AS THEIR FAVOURITE TIPPLE.

Inspiration for costumes could come from: Bahama Mama, Black Russian, Bloody Mary, Blue Lady, B-52, Devils, Fluffy Duck, Green Pixie, The Morning After, Moulin Rouge, Moscow Mule, Pink Lady, TNT, or a Zombie.

For a double-strength gin and tonic, add ice cubes made from G&T set with lemon slices to the drink.

BRING A COCKTAIL PARTY

PHOTOCOPY SOME FAVOURITE COCKTAIL RECIPES AND ASK GUESTS TO BRING ALONG THE INGREDIENTS.

Reduce the cocktail recipes to the size of a postcard, paste them to the back of tropical scenes, and send them out as invitations. You supply the garnishes, ice cubes, umbrellas, stirrers, fruit and, of course, the food.

◁ VODKA PARTY

★ Freeze bottles of flavoured vodka for at least six hours. The alcohol level prevents the vodka from freezing solid.

★ Mix jugs of vodka-based Sea Breezes (*see page 90*), Bloody Marys and Moscow Mules in advance. Just add ice to the jugs as your guests arrive.

★ Set jellies made with vodka in pots or tequila shot glasses (*see left*). Cool in the fridge and serve with spoons.

CUTLERY-FREE DINING

THE BEST TYPE OF FOOD to serve at a cocktail party is small, bite-sized items that can be easily eaten without a knife, fork or plate. Offer canapés (*see menu, above*), one-bite sandwiches, melon or figs wrapped in Parma ham, satay sticks, crudités, chips and dips. Serve food on trays garnished with vine leaves, and hand out napkins as you circulate.

HOT TODDIES

GLÜHWEIN, JÄGERTEE, SWEDISH GLOGG (SEE PAGE 43), MULLED WINE (SEE PAGE 91) AND IRISH COFFEE ARE THE PERFECT DRINKS TO SERVE AT AN APRÉS–SKI PARTY.

To make Irish Coffee, add a single measure of whisky to a cup of black coffee. Then float the cream on top by holding a teaspoon, bowl side up, just above the coffee and slowly pouring the cream over it into the cup.

ON THE ROCKS ▷

ONE OF THE SIMPLEST WAYS TO GARNISH A COCKTAIL IS WITH DECORATIVE ICE CUBES. TRY SOME OF THE FOLLOWING IDEAS:

Stir a little food colouring into the water before freezing; use shaped ice-cube trays; add slices of olive, strawberry, orange, lime, mint leaves and edible fresh flower petals to the ice-cube tray (*see right*); or simply present ice to guests in a pretty ice bowl (*see page 66*).

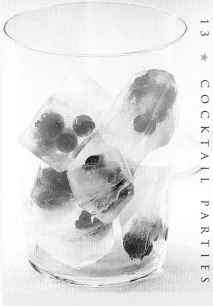

BOOZY LOLLIES

COOL YOUR SUMMER GUESTS WITH ALCOHOLIC LOLLIES.

Stir together in a bowl a mixture of champagne or sparkling wine, sugar, water and a little blackcurrant vodka to taste. Pour into lolly moulds and freeze. Variations of this lolly can be made using piña colada, daiquiri or margarita cocktails (*see page 90*) that have been sweetened to taste then frozen.

To make crystal-clear ice cubes, always freeze filtered or bottled water.

FROSTING GLASSES

DRINKS SUCH AS MARGARITAS ARE TRADITIONALLY SERVED IN GLASSES WITH FROSTED RIMS.

To frost a glass with salt, dip the rim of the glass in lemon or lime juice before lightly dipping it in salt. For sugar- or sherbet-frosted glasses, dip the rim of the glass in beaten egg white, then into caster sugar or sherbet. Look out for brightly coloured sherbet in confectionery shops.

FRILLS & FLOUNCES

HOME–MADE COCKTAILS LOOK MORE COLOURFUL AND PROFESSIONAL IF THEY ARE SERVED WITH A GARNISH, BENDY STRAW OR STIRRER.

Stirrers are vital for some cocktails because spirits and soft drinks do not mix and must therefore be stirred well. Always serve Bloody Marys with a celery stick stirrer.

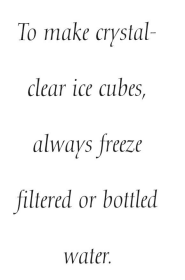

PINEAPPLE SHELLS

GIVE COCKTAILS A TROPICAL FEEL BY SERVING THEM IN HOLLOWED–OUT PINEAPPLES OR COCONUT SHELLS.

To make a pineapple shell, trim off one-third of the leafy end of a pineapple and discard. Cut a thin slice from the base, so it sits level. Using a small, sharp knife, cut around the inside edge of the pineapple, leaving a 1cm (½in) rim. Scoop out the centre and fill it with a tropical drink.

CRUSHED & CRACKED ICE

WHITE RUSSIANS, ZOMBIES AND FRAPPÉS ARE BEST SERVED OVER CRACKED ICE.

To crack ice, wrap the ice in a clean tea towel, and hit it carefully with a mallet or rolling pin. To crush more finely, simply hit it for longer. Some, but not all, food processors can crush ice, so check the instructions first. Crack any large ice cubes before processing.

SPEND LONG DAYS PARTYING BY THE BEACH, POOL OR LAKE,

PLAYING VOLLEYBALL AND EATING ICE CREAM, SEAFOOD AND POPCORN.

INVITE FRIENDS TO A SUNSET PICNIC AND SERVE A FEAST FROM

WICKER BASKETS IN AN AREA SURROUNDED WITH TINY CANDLES.

HOLD A PARTY FULL OF EASTERN PROMISE, INVITING GUESTS

OUTDOOR PARTIES

TO RECLINE ON CUSHIONS UNDER A TENTED CANOPY

OUTDOORS. ON BALMY SUMMER EVENINGS HANG THE

TREES WITH FAIRY LIGHTS OR HURRICANE LAMPS, AND ENJOY NIGHTS

FILLED WITH CAMPFIRES, SLUMBER PARTIES AND

MIDNIGHT FEASTS. AFTER SUPPER, PLAY NOISY, BOISTEROUS

GAMES, AND END BY TELLING STORIES AND SINGING AROUND THE FIRE.

SUMMER PARTIES

SERVE CANDY FLOSS, ICE LOLLIES,
COLD BEERS AND FRUIT PUNCHES,
AND FOR A DELICIOUS SUMMER
DRINK, DROP TWO RASPBERRIES IN
A CHAMPAGNE FLUTE, COVER WITH A
MEASURE OF CASSIS, AND TOP UP
WITH CHILLED CHAMPAGNE.
GARNISH WITH A STRAWBERRY.

SOUTH PACIFIC PARTY ▷

CREATE A BEACH IN YOUR BACK GARDEN, THEN HULA
HULA AND SWAY THE NIGHT AWAY TO THE STRAINS
OF A TONGAN BEAT AND THE MUSIC OF *SOUTH PACIFIC*.

Invite Attach an invitation to silk flowers threaded into
garlands (*see right*). Tell guests to come in swimwear and
grass skirts, and to paddle to the party in canoes.

Decor Create stretches of shore using sand and shells.
Hang trees with lights (*see page 39*), scatter the garden with
petals, and set up the food under a canopy (*see right*).

Table Cover tables with crêpe paper, strewn
with petals. Fill terracotta pots with orchids and
tie cutlery into bundles with raffia (*see right*).

Food Spread platters with vine leaves, and heap
with prawns, crab claws and barbecued fish. Serve
daiquiri- and margarita-flavoured ice lollies (*see page 13*),
coconut ice cream and tropical fruit salad (*see page 113*).

Drinks Offer cocktails in pineapple shells (*page 13*).

PARTY IN THE PARK

THROUGHOUT SUMMER, LOCAL HISTORICAL SITES AND
PARKS HOLD OUTDOOR EVENTS. ENJOY THE ENTERTAINMENT
WITH FRIENDS AND WITH SOME DELICIOUS FOOD.

Invite Ask everyone to bring an allotted dish from a menu,
a drinks ingredient, something to sit on, cutlery, and plates.

Table Bring chequered blankets to lay the food on. Tie a
helium balloon to a bottle, so friends can find you.

Food Chips, dips and canapés (*see pages 86–89*), rustic breads
and summer salads (*see right*). Serve strawberries dipped in
chocolate with cream. Take a selection of cheeses, some flasks
of steaming coffee and mints to finish.

Scour the garden for small blooms

and pretty leaves, then tuck

them under the edge of

each place mat a few

minutes before guests arrive.

SUMMER PARTY MENU

CHARGRILLED CHICKEN WITH FIGS (*SEE PAGE 99*)

MINTED POTATO SALAD (*SEE PAGE 104*)

PESTO COUSCOUS SALAD (*SEE PAGE 105*)

SUMMER SALAD

Scatter a salad with edible flowers such as nasturtiums, geraniums, borage, rose or marigold petals. Pick fresh, unsprayed and unblemished blooms, and check carefully for insects before washing.

●

SUMMER BERRY TARTS (*SEE PAGE 112*)

TENTED CANOPY

A CANOPY CAN BE USED AS A DELIGHTFUL SETTING FOR AN OUTDOOR MEAL, AS A CENTRAL BASE CAMP FOR A DAY OUT WITH FRIENDS, OR EVEN AS AN EXOTIC SHELTER ON A HOT SUMMER NIGHT.

Make a simple tented canopy by driving tall stakes into the ground and wrapping them with strips of wide, thick ribbon. Dye a cotton sheet and tie it to the top of the stakes, leaving the knotted ends to trail down at each corner. Decorate the corners with organza bows, swags of foliage and ribbons.

SUMMER SLUMBER PARTY

CHILDREN LOVE CAMPING, SO INVITE FAMILIES TO PITCH THEIR TENTS IN YOUR BACK GARDEN AND ENJOY MIDNIGHT FEASTS AROUND A CAMPFIRE.

Invite Send out invitations attached to packets of marshmallows, telling children to bring along a skewer to toast them on. Remind guests also to bring a change of clothes, a sleeping bag and a toothbrush.

Decor Pitch tents and light a campfire with adult supervision. Stand nightlights in glass jars, tie string around them as handles, and hang them from trees and shrubs. Set up trestle tables and cover with paper cloths. Serve food in billy-cans with disposable cutlery.

Food Serve hot dogs or ribs with fried onions and cheesy jacket potatoes (*see page 106*). Toast marshmallows and teacakes and wash them down with creamy hot chocolate.

Games Play lots of loud, energetic games. Try touch tag, musical bumps and hide and seek. Finish with Chinese whispers (*see pages 72*) and campfire songs.

MAKING HAY PICNIC

THIS IS THE BEST PARTY TO HOLD WHEN THE WEATHER IS SURE TO BE FINE. MEET UP IN THE COUNTRYSIDE, ERECT A CANOPY AS BASE CAMP (*SEE LEFT*), PUT SOFT DRINKS ON ICE, AND SPEND THE DAY PLAYING GAMES AND PICNICKING IN THE SUN – THINK *OKLAHOMA*.

Invite Call up your friends and invite them to bring along the whole family, a picnic lunch, and even the dog.

Table Use bales of hay as tables and chairs.

Food Tell everyone to bring their own picnic while you supply the soft drinks. Keep the drinks chilled in a dustbin full of ice. Mix Bucks Fizz (*see page 90*) in a sterilized picnic box and let everyone help themselves.

Games Set up nets and play volleyball, football, softball and Frisbee; take a whistle and run races; go on a nature hunt and collect butterflies and bugs in glass jars.

Must pack Bring large plastic sacks for rubbish and a small first-aid kit in case of accidents.

BARBECUES

BARBECUED FOOD TASTES EVEN MORE DELICIOUS WHEN FLAVOURED WITH SMOKE. DO THIS BY SPRINKLING ANY OF THE FOLLOWING ON HOT COALS: FRESH HERBS, SUCH AS ROSEMARY OR THYME; APPLE-TREE WOOD; SOAKED WOOD CHIPS FROM WHISKY, MAPLE OR OAK BARRELS; CRACKED ALMOND OR HAZELNUT SHELLS, FIRST SOAKED IN WATER FOR 20 MINUTES.

MONGOLIAN BARBECUE

LET GUESTS PICK AND MIX THEIR OWN FOOD BEFORE YOU COOK IT FOR THEM ON A RED–HOT GRIDDLE.

Decor Hang tin-can lights (*see page 39*) in the trees.

Table Cover a large table and surrounding area with fat church candles. If you are short of seats, place a plank of wood between two flat seats, and use it as a bench.

Food Serve food in large bowls with chopsticks. Provide a wide range of fresh ingredients, such as sliced chicken, prawns, meats, chopped vegetables, sauces, herbs and spices, all in separate bowls. To help guests decide what to eat, paste photocopied recipes around the eating area, and encourage them to try different options, and also to experiment with their own concoctions. Serve the food with bowls of salad, stir-fried rice, noodles and a selection of bread.

PREPARING the COALS

1 Lay coals on a foil-lined barbecue tray, two-deep and slightly wider than the cooking area. Make a pyramid of coals in the middle, push a firelighter into this and light it.

2 Wait until the flames die down and the coals glow; this can take 45 minutes. Rake the coals evenly over the base.

3 Brush the grill rack with oil. Place food over the hottest part of the coals to seal it before moving it to a cooler part of the rack in order to cook it thoroughly.

BARBECUE EQUIPMENT

ESSENTIAL EQUIPMENT for a successful barbecue includes: long-handled tongs, basting brush, oven mitts, skewers, hinged wire rack for sausages, fish rack, long fork, lighter fuel, charcoal and firelighters.

BARBECUE MENU

BRUSCHETTA WITH TOPPINGS (*SEE PAGE 89*)

•

LAMB BURGERS (*SEE PAGE 101*)

MONKFISH & BACON KEBABS (*SEE PAGE 101*)

TUSCAN BEAN SALAD (*SEE PAGE 104*)

ANTIPASTO PASTA SALAD (*SEE PAGE 105*)

•

CHOCOLATE TART (*SEE PAGE 108*)

•

JUGS OF BUCK'S FIZZ (*SEE PAGE 90*)

PASSION FRUIT MIX (*SEE PAGE 91*)

A SELECTION OF BEERS

YAHOO PARTY

RECREATE THE DAYS OF THE GOLD RUSH AND ENJOY A RAUCOUS EVENING OF WILD WEST ACTION.

Invite Attach a label to a sheriff's badge or toy gun.

Costumes Calamity Jane, Buffalo Bill, The Lone Ranger.

Decor Surround a campfire with hay bales, hang hurricane lamps in the trees, and pitch tents for guests to sleep over in. Serve food from an improvized chuck wagon.

Music Hand out yazoos or combs and papers, and busk along to your favourite country-and-western songs.

Food Serve buckets of beans, coleslaw, grits, cornbread (*see page 88*), spicy chicken wings and seared tuna (*see page 100*). For dessert, stuff bananas with chocolate and bake in the fire's embers (*see page 24*).

Entertainment Set up an area for line-dancing.

Games Hold a toy gun shooting contest using tin cans, a horseshoe throwing competition, lassooing and poker.

◁ LAZY SUMMER BARBECUE

SOME OF THE BEST PARTIES HAPPEN OUT OF THE BLUE, SO IF THE WEATHER IS BALMY ONE DAY, THROW AN IMPROMPTU BARBECUE IN THE GARDEN OR BY A LAKE.

Decor Make petal flares out of drinks cans (*see left*). Clean a can with paint stripper and wire wool, then cut the top off using strong scissors. Cut the sides of the can into six "petals", and bend them back around a pencil. Remove a night-light from its metal surround, place the surround in the can, and hammer a long nail through both layers of metal, into the pithy end of a garden cane. Secure the nail with glue, replace the night-light and push the flare into a bucket of sand.

Table Cover the table with brown paper, and provide crayons to play word games after the meal.

Games Play two-man bluff. Divide guests into two groups, and blindfold a player from each team. One player has to catch the other, while the second player tries to get away, both following directions shouted by their teams.

PICNICS

FOR A GREAT PICNIC, PACK FOOD
THAT IS EASILY EATEN WITH FINGERS.
PLACE ICE PACKS ON TOP; COLD
AIR WILL FALL AND KEEP FOOD COOL.
USE SMALL SCREW-TOP JARS FOR
DRESSINGS AND FREEZE BOTTLES
OF FRUIT JUICE, SO IT IS COLD ON
ARRIVAL. DON'T FORGET DUSTBIN
BAGS, CONDIMENTS, HAND WIPES
AND A CORKSCREW.

TEDDY BEARS' PICNIC

TELL EVERYONE TO BRING THEIR TEDDY BEARS TO JOIN
IN THE FUN AT THIS PICNIC. ALL BEARS MUST WEAR
A LABEL WITH THEIR OWNER'S NAME.

Invite Send on labels attached to small teddy bears.

Costumes Get a couple of guests to come as famous
bears, such as Winnie the Pooh, Paddington or Yogi Bear.

Decor Hold the party in a large field or set it in a sunny
spot in the woods. Picnic on gingham tablecloths, or
make a padded mat (*see page 80*).

Food Serve savoury scones with
toppings (*see page 88*), a floral summer
salad (*see page 17*), summer berry
tarts (*see page 112*), blueberry
muffins (*see page 114*) and a huge
teddy bear cake (*see page 117*).

Games Hide and seek,
rounders, sing songs, Frisbee.

FRUIT-PICKING PARTY

SPEND A DAY WITH FAMILY AND FRIENDS ON A FARM
WHERE YOU CAN PICK YOUR OWN FRUIT.

Food Ask everyone to bring a different course. Eat the picnic
together with fresh produce such as butter and honey
produced at the farm. For dessert, eat some of the fresh fruit
you have picked with cream from the farm.

Entertainment Enjoy tractor rides and visit the farm animals.

Games Set children a challenge to hunt the
largest strawberry, or to find the longest or
strangest-looking vegetable.

PICNIC ON THE PISTE

TAKE RUCKSACKS AND A PICNIC, AND ENJOY A MORNING'S
SKIING BEFORE TUCKING INTO A HEARTY LUNCH.

Table Ski to a picnic site straight away and bury drinks and
food in the snow, wrapped in plastic bags. Also bury paper
plates, napkins and plastic cutlery in bags. Mark the spot.

Food Bring food already cut into portions. Pack it in seal-
tight plastic boxes that are resilient to knocks and bumps.

Entertainment Have fun skiing all morning before finding
your picnic spot at lunch time. Sit on plastic bags to keep
dry, and enjoy a meal washed down with ice-cold drinks.

Paint olives and leaves on to napkins and tablecloths using fabric paints, then fix the design with a hot iron.

FOURTH OF JULY

ENJOY THE FOURTH OF JULY WITH AN ALL–AMERICAN CELEBRATION. PLAN A DAY OF ACTIVITIES, STARTING WITH A PICNIC FOR FRIENDS, AND FINISHING WITH A RED, WHITE AND BLUE FIREWORK DISPLAY.

Invite Attach to mini American flags, or send out on the back of Uncle Sam postcards.

Costumes Invite guests to come dressed as different states – all 52 of them.

Decor Red paper plates and white napkins, blue paper cups and plastic cutlery. Paint red and blue stripes using fabric paint on a plain white tablecloth, then spray on silver or white stars using a stencil. Iron to fix the design.

Food Offer mini picnic pies (*see page 97*), cold, boned stuffed turkey (*see page 103*), minted potato salad and rocket salad (*see page 104*), mini pecan pies and rich chocolate cheesecake (*see page 109*).

Entertainment Enjoy a game of softball or baseball and finish the day with a firework display.

◁ ## TUSCAN PICNIC

WHEN FLOWERS ARE IN FULL BLOOM AND CROPS ARE RIPENING, HEAD OUT FOR A DAY IN THE COUNTRYSIDE BEFORE EATING A SUNSET TUSCAN FEAST.

Invite Write invitations directly on to paper plates, and decorate them with painted sunflowers.

Decor Dot tiny cake-tin candles (*see left*) around the picnic area, and light them at sunset.

Table Pack up traditional picnic hampers with terracotta plates and wooden bowls. Plant fragrant herbs in terracotta pots, then stud the pots with coloured tapers. Line the herb pots down the centre of the picnic area. Roll napkins and tie a sunflower to each one with ribbon.

Food Simple but delicious: ciabatta and focaccia breads, herby garlic mixed olives (*see page 89*), salami, treacle glazed ham (*see page 102*), tuscan bean salad (*see page 104*), antipasto pasta salad (*see page 105*), poached peaches (*see page 111*), and a selection of Italian cheeses. Serve with an Italian wine, such as Chianti, Frascati or Pinot Grigio.

PERFECT PICNIC TIPS

★ Cake-tin candles, dotted around an eating area at dusk, look enchanting. Use small, old cake tins, madeleine cases or pastry moulds. Glue the bases of two tins together to make a candle holder on a stand. Sit a night-light inside each top tin, and position the candles around the picnic area.

★ Tie seashells, small stones with holes in them, or knives and forks on to lengths of string, and criss-cross over a picnic tablecloth, to keep it in place when the wind blows.

★ Make a picnic place mat for each diner. Lay a paper napkin on a quilted place mat. Put a knife, fork, spoon and disposable hand wipe on top. Roll up the mat and tie with ribbon.

◁

TENNIS TEA

EVEN IF YOU CAN'T BE THERE, YOU DON'T HAVE TO MISS OUT ON THE FUN AND EXCITEMENT OF WIMBLEDON.

Invite Attach a card to a tennis ball, reminding guests to bring sun hats, visors, sunglasses and plenty of sunblock.

Decor Set up a television outdoors with a line of director's chairs in front, then sit back and relax with a grandstand view. Serve food using daisy-chain napkins (*see left and page 78*).

Food Fill bowls with strawberries and cream.

Drinks Pimm's (*see page 90*), fruit purées with sparkling water.

Games If children can't sit still, set up a game of Swingball.

GARDEN PARTIES

ENJOY A REFINED AFTERNOON IN A BEAUTIFUL GARDEN, DRINKING CHAMPAGNE AND EATING STRAWBERRIES AND CREAM.

GREEN FINGER PARTY

IN EARLY SPRING, invite friends for an afternoon swapping cuttings, trading seeds and exchanging tips before settling down for a talk by a local garden-centre expert. This is a great party to hold in a greenhouse or large conservatory. Tell guests to bring problem plants for the expert's opinion.

GARDEN TIDY PARTY

IF YOU HAVE MOVED HOUSE, or have an elderly relative who needs help taming their garden, throw a garden-tidy party. Send invites on seed packets, asking guests to bring tools. Keep everyone refreshed with lemonade, and send them home with small bottles of massage oil for tired limbs.

RAINFOREST SAFARI

COME AS EXPLORERS, archaeologists, Indiana Jones or characters from *The Jungle Book*. Play a rainforest tape for background music and rendezvous in a steamy conservatory full of plants.

CROQUET PARTY

MOW THE LAWN, tidy up the flower beds, and set up hoops for an afternoon of croquet. Transform old garden furniture with daisy prints (*see page 80*), erect parasols or canopies (*see page 17*) for guests to sit beneath, and enjoy an afternoon tea of sandwiches and dainties (*see pages 114–15*). For the less agile, set up card tables on a terrace.

PAMPERED POOCH PARTY

ON HIS OR HER BIRTHDAY, INVITE ALL YOUR PET'S BEST DOGGY PALS TO AN AFTERNOON OF PAMPERING.

Invite Tie to a pack of doggy chocolate drops.

Decor Cushions for lounging, videos of dog shows and *Lassie*, or cartoons of *Tom and Jerry*.

Food Nothing but the best: steak gently braised, hearts, chicken and any other favourites, plus a meaty cake.

Entertainment Hire a dog beautician to groom and beautify your precious pooches.

PARTIES AFLOAT

TIE INVITATIONS TO POTS OF BUBBLES,
TELLING GUESTS TO BRING SWIMMING
COSTUMES AND PLENTY OF TOWELS, AS
NO ONE IS GOING TO STAY DRY!

TWILIGHT SAILING

CHOOSE A SUMMER'S NIGHT with a full moon, and set sail across the harbour at dusk. Make cake-tin candles (*see page 21*) to illuminate the deck, and bring cushions and throws for guests to lounge on. If you or your friends don't have a boat, set hurricane lamps up on the jetty and have the party there instead!

TUBING PARTY

IF YOU DON'T OWN A BOAT, the cheapest option for a party afloat is to use old tyre inner tubes and float down a shallow, slow-moving stream with friends. Float towards a car full of dry clothes, towels, drinks and plenty of food.

MISSISSIPPI STEAMER

RELIVE THE DAYS OF *HUCKLEBERRY FINN*, AND CHARTER A PADDLE STEAMER ON YOUR FAVOURITE STRETCH OF RIVER.

Costumes Invite guests to come dressed as saloon girls, riverboat gamblers and characters from *Gone with the Wind*.

Music Rousing saloon-bar music played on the piano.

Food Serve smoked chicken (*see page 98*), grits, hickory ribs, cornbread (*see page 88*) and chocolate tart (*see page 108*).

Drinks Offer beer, bourbon and Southern Comfort.

Entertainment Hire dancing saloon girls and install croupiers behind gaming tables.

SUMMER SPLASH

SHOW THE CHILDREN A SPLASHING GOOD TIME WITH A PARTY SET AROUND A POOL.

Invite Send out team swimming caps in two different colours for children to customize as they wish (*see below*).

Decor Hang tyres from the trees, float a flock of rubber ducks on the pool, throw treasure to the bottom and float as many inflatables as possible.

Games Water volleyball, swimming races, diving for treasure, water tag and the biggest water pistol fight ever. Set up paddling pools or use rubber rings for children who can't swim, and supervise everyone at all times.

GIRLS AFLOAT

A CANAL OR RIVER BOAT IS THE IDEAL PLACE TO SPEND A WEEKEND'S HEN PARTY; THERE IS NO NEED TO WATCH THE CLOCK, AND YOU CAN COME AND GO AS YOU PLEASE.

Invite Try to keep the party a surprise; the bride-to-be should not suspect what is being planned.

Drinks Champagne, of course.

Entertainment Every guest has to bring a small gift for the bride. Set the bride ten fun challenges, such as getting someone to buy her a drink, and take Polaroid pictures of her completing these, to mount in a signed keepsake album.

BEACH PARTIES

THINK BONDI, MONTEGO BAY, HAWAII.
DRESS AS SEA NYMPHS OR LIFEGUARDS,
AND DANCE THE NIGHT AWAY
TO A STEEL DRUM BAND.

EATING IN STYLE ▷

★ Create a sandcastle centrepiece for the dining area by filling a shallow dish or large plastic bowl with sand. Build a sandcastle in the middle and decorate the centrepiece with shells and starfish (*see right*).

★ Inexpensive camping ground sheets make excellent picnic mats when faced with thick canvas. For a seaside feel, print the canvas with a pebble effect (*see page 80*).

★ For an instant canopy effect that is ideal for children's parties, spread dry towels out to form a huge picnic mat. Stand bamboo canes at the corners and link them together with streamers and balloons.

TIPS FOR A WORRY-FREE DAY

★ If you are enjoying an evening barbecue on the beach, keep worrying insects at bay by lighting citronella candles and wiping exposed skin with lavender water.

★ Keep babies and young children safe from the sun by taking a small, easy-to-assemble tent to the beach. This shelters children from harmful rays, offers a sand-free area where they can play with toys, and provides somewhere for you to change them.

★ Ensure that children wear cotton plimsolls or jelly sandals to protect their feet from hot sand and sharp rocks that can be hidden in the water.

POTATO BAKE

MEET WITH FRIENDS WHILE IT IS STILL LIGHT, AND COLLECT KINDLING FOR A ROARING BONFIRE.

Build a fire and bury foil-wrapped potatoes in the embers. Bring plenty of fillings, along with butter, salt and pepper, paper plates and napkins. To keep drinks cool, place cans and bottles in a large string bag, anchor it to the shore and let the water wash over it. Finish by eating baked bananas: cut through the banana skins, stuff them with chocolate, wrap in foil and place in the embers until the chocolate melts to a delicious goo.

TREASURE ISLAND PARTY

FLY THE JOLLY ROGER AND HEAD FOR A SANDY BEACH TO ENJOY A DAY OF SWASHBUCKLING PIRATE FUN.

Invite Attach to black eye patches or pirate hats.

Costumes Dress as Long John Silver or his parrot, Captain Hook, Blackbeard, Peter Pan or Tinkerbell.

Decor Pack up "treasure-chest" picnic hampers, with food tied in red and white spotted napkins. Paint beach mats (*see page 80*) with a skull and crossbones.

Games Hide clues and treasure for children and hand out maps. Set up a start and finish line for races.

BESIDE THE SEASIDE CELEBRATION

HIRE A MINIBUS, PACK IT WITH KIDS, AND HEAD FOR THE BEACH FOR A BIRTHDAY PARTY WITH A DIFFERENCE.

Invite Tie a label to sunglasses, asking children to bring dry clothes, sun hat, sunblock, towel and bathing costume.

Food Filled bagels, fresh fruit, crudités and popcorn.

Games Give each child a party bag with a bucket and spade, a fishing net, paper flags and a glass jar threaded with string. Rock-pool for fish and shrimps, then build a sandcastle big enough to picnic in.

GAMES FOR THE BEACH

DIVIDE GUESTS INTO TEAMS, PRESENT EACH WITH PERSONALIZED TEAM T-SHIRTS, THEN COMMENCE AN AFTERNOON OF BEACH OLYMPICS WITH SOME OF THE FOLLOWING GAMES:

Softball ★ Supersoaker water pistols ★ French cricket
Beach crazy golf ★ Noughts and crosses in the sand
Tug of war ★ Volleyball ★ Diablos ★ Boules ★ Kite flying
Sand sculpting ★ Water fights ★ Hopscotch ★ Quoits
Frisbee ★ Leap-frog ★ Water relay
Touch tag ★ Inflatable races
Swimming races ★ Football

MIDNIGHT DIP

FOR A MAGICAL NIGHT-TIME DIP, time this party to take place under a full moon. Build a campfire to warm up by afterwards, and have flasks of hot chocolate on standby. At the stroke of twelve o'clock, throw caution to the wind and take the plunge.

NEW YEAR'S DAY DIP

CLEAR OUT CHRISTMAS cobwebs with a dip in the ocean on New Year's Day. Meet up with friends on the beach, equipped with soft drinks, bars of chocolate to replenish energy levels and plenty of dry towels. Then take a dip, if only up to your ankles!

BEACH PARTY WINDMILLS

ARRANGE THESE BRIGHTLY COLOURED WINDMILLS AROUND A PARTY AREA SO THAT GUESTS CAN FIND YOU.

Cut sheets of colourful paper into squares of the same size, and glue co-ordinated colours together in pairs. When dry, cut diagonally from each corner almost into the centre; the paper will look like four joined triangles. Punch a hole through the centre of the square and through alternate outside corners of the triangles. Fold the punched corners into the centre of the square, one after the other. Thread a paper fastener through the layers of paper, then thread through a hole in the top of a bamboo cane and fasten.

Anchor tablecloths with pretty sandcastles, or piles of rocks and seashells. Then serve a feast from colourful china plates.

GETTING MARRIED OPENS UP A WHOLE WORLD OF EXCITING PARTY POSSIBILITIES. TAKE A CLASSIC THEME SUCH AS SUMMER FLORALS, AND STYLE THE DRESS, FLOWERS, INVITATIONS AND DECOR TO MATCH, OR BREAK WITH TRADITION AND ADOPT A MODERN MOTIF WITH BRIGHT, TRANSLUCENT COLOUR OR A

BANQUETS & WEDDINGS

GLAMOROUS COSTUME THEME. DON'T CONFINE EXTRAVAGANT LARGE-SCALE PARTIES TO WEDDINGS – THROW A BALL IN A SPLENDID LOCATION TO CELEBRATE A GROUP OF FRIENDS' BIRTHDAYS, A RETIREMENT OR GRADUATION, OR PLAN A MAGICAL BANQUET IN A SILK-SWATHED MARQUEE FOR A FANTASTIC FAMILY REUNION OR BON VOYAGE BASH. A FEAST OF IDEAS FOLLOWS.

Moorish Feast

SET THIS PARTY IN A MARQUEE FILLED WITH SILK HANGINGS AND MAGIC CARPETS. LIGHT THE TENT WITH BRASS LAMPS AND SCENT IT WITH JASMINE INCENSE.

Invite Send attached to a packet of incense sticks.

Costumes Belly dancers, bedouins, sultans and sultanas, Aladdin, genies, and magic carpets.

Decor Decorate walls with hangings (*see below*), and arrange low seating so that guests can lounge. Cover table tops with paper mosaics (*see page 77*).

Food Serve food from platters lined with banana leaves. Offer kebabs, pesto couscous salad (*see page 105*), coconut ice cream (*see page 113*) and Turkish delight.

Drinks Sherbet, mint tea and strong coffee.

Entertainment Magicians, snake charmers and belly dancers. Paint wooden boards with people riding carpets; cut out the faces, set them up and invite guests to stand behind and pose for photographs as they arrive.

Customize plain Venetian masks by painting them with poster or emulsion paint. Trim the edges with braiding, or stick on sequins, beads, organza and tulle.

Moorish Hangings

CREATE A SENSE OF OPULENCE by hanging silk saris, dyed muslin or crushed velvet around the walls of a room. For a truly luxurious effect, embellish the cloth by adding intricate designs to the fabric with gold metallic paint. The cloth can be further adorned with fake gems, and the edges trimmed with gold bobble braiding.

Venetian Tablecloths

TO MAKE HARLEQUIN CLOTHS, fold white tablecloths into quarters, or into eighths if the tablecloths are large. Paint a black diamond in opposite quarters (or eighths) using fabric paint. When the paint is dry, iron the cloth to fix the design.

Gold-swirled Glasses

TRANSFORM INEXPENSIVE GLASSES by adding a touch of colour with a swirl or two of glass paint. Buy some cheap, plain glasses, making sure they are clean and dry before painting. Draw a name or design on the glass using gold relief paint, then allow the design to dry.

Venetian Masquerade Ball

HOST AN EXTRAVAGANT, ELEGANT PARTY IN A GRAND VENUE, WITH GUESTS DISGUISED BEHIND MASKS.

Invite Send plain black masks through the post asking the recipients to customize and decorate them to suit their outfits.

Costumes Pierrots, shepherdesses, 18th-century gentlemen, circus performers and gondoliers. Dress up with white make-up, beauty spots, powdered wigs, hooped skirts, fans and handkerchief sleeves, white tights, high buckle shoes, lace, satin and brocade.

Decor Hang elegant mirrors and grand-looking chandeliers. Serve supper on Venetian Harlequin tablecloths (*see left*) and drink wine from gold-swirled glasses (*see left*).

Music Harpsichord, and a string quartet for minuets.

Entertainment Present all female guests with a dance card to fill in for the evening. Insist that, as the clock strikes midnight, everyone joins the dance floor to remove their masks and reveal their true identities.

Olde English Banquet

ENJOY AN EVENING OF REVELRY IN A BARN OR OLD HALL. SET TABLES IN A LONG HORSESHOE SHAPE AND SIT THE PRINCIPAL GUESTS AT THE HEAD, AS THE LORD AND LADY.

Invite Write in old English script then tear the edges, age by dipping in strong, cold tea, and roll and tie with red ribbon.

Costumes Anything from the era of Elizabeth I: Sir Walter Raleigh, Mary Queen of Scots, monks, friars and peasants.

Decor Trestle tables and benches, with thrones for the lord and lady (*see below*). Serve food from wooden platters (*see below*) and drink ale from flagons. Use beeswax candles, scatter the floor with reeds or straw, and hang garlands from the ceiling.

Food Eat by hand but allow guests knives. Serve rustic bread, treacle glazed ham (*see page 102*), roast chicken, chocolate tart (*see page 108*), platters of cheese and bowls of fruits and nuts.

Entertainment Hire a juggler, flame thrower and lute player.

Games Make stocks to imprison naughty guests' arms and legs, tell bawdy jokes and dance the galliard.

Midsummer Night's Ball

OPEN YOUR GARDEN FOR A MIDSUMMER NIGHT'S EVE PARTY UNDER THE STARS. DRESS CHILDREN AS FAIRIES, AND HAVE THEM HAND OUT GARLANDS OF HERBS TO WARD OFF MISCHIEVOUS SPIRITS.

Invite Send invitations attached to packets of sparklers, for guests to use as fairy wands on the night.

Costumes Dress as Titania, Oberon or Puck, or as spirits, imps, pixies and fairies with silver wings.

Decor Hang trees with white fairy lights, crystals, tiny bells and wind chimes. Decorate tables with garlands of fresh herbs and flowers, and seat guests on ivy heart chairs (*see below*). Fill the air with the aroma of scented candles, essential oils and scattered petals, and create a mystical feel with a dry ice or bubble machine.

Entertainment Dress a musician as Pan, and create a fairy bower in which he can play his pipes. Hire fortune tellers and magicians, and a violinist to serenade diners. End the evening with a bonfire and fireworks.

Olde English Throne

CREATE REGAL SEATING by turning chairs into thrones for a lord and lady. Cut a throne back from thick card or plywood to a desired shape, and spray gold. Punch a hole on each side of the throne back, thread with ribbon and attach to the front of a chair, tying the ribbons behind. Cover the seat in velvet and set with fake jewels.

Olde English Platter

SERVE FOOD ON WOODEN BOARDS for a truly Elizabethan touch. Have a local wood merchant cut out discs about 40cm (15½in) in diameter, then seal the wood with varnish to give a washable surface.

◁ Midsummer Ivy Heart Chair

TIE EVERGREEN HEARTS to the backs of chairs for a magical, midsummer feel. Gather long lengths of ivy, and twist and secure them around heart-shaped wire templates, about 15cm (6in) in diameter. Tie each heart with a long ribbon and hang it on the back of a chair. You can attach a place setting card to each heart.

WONDERLAND BALL

ENJOY A MAD, UPSIDE DOWN, BACK–TO–FRONT EVENING IN TRUE LEWIS CARROLL STYLE.

Invite Write the invitation backwards, so guests have to read it through a looking glass (*see below*).

Costumes The Queen of Hearts, the Mad Hatter, the White Rabbit, the Dormouse, Tweedledum and Tweedledee, the Walrus, the Caterpillar, Alice and the Cheshire Cat.

Decor Stand fake pink flamingoes in a pond. Hang huge playing cards on walls, and arrange flowers in upturned top hats. Cover tables with blue and white checked cloths, and tie a heart-shaped gas balloon to every chair.

Food Serve a grand high tea buffet (*see pages 114–15*) with food and drink labelled "eat me" and "drink me". Drink tea after the meal and serve liqueurs in fake medicine bottles.

Entertainment Place distorting mirrors at the entrance of the venue that make guests grow or shrink. Dance the quadrille, organize a walking poet to recite to guests, and someone to perform card tricks. Play croquet after tea.

EGYPTIAN EXTRAVAGANZA

TRAVEL BACK IN TIME TO THE 1920S, WHEN THE TREASURES OF THE TOMB OF TUTANKHAMUN WERE UNCOVERED.

Invite Written on hand-made paper with a painted border of hieroglyphics around the edges.

Costumes Cleopatra, mummies, sphinxes, priestesses, scribes, khaki-dressed explorers, loin cloths, loose robes, thonged sandals, heavy kohl-rimmed eyes, gold and heavy jewellery.

Decor Create your own Egyptian tomb, straight from the Valley of the Kings. Paint huge murals depicting pyramids, dancers, musicians, scarab beetles and the gods Isis and Osiris. Stand "ancient" vases, oil lamps and scrolls around the room. Complete the look with archeologists' spades, old cameras, pith helmets, maps and binoculars. Make papier-mâché pyramids or sphinxes and put them by the front door.

Music Harp, flute and lyre music, or groups of Egyptian or Nubian musicians.

Entertainment Spread sand on the dance floor and encourage guests to do a sand dance.

LOOKING GLASS INVITES ▷

TO MAKE BACK–TO–FRONT INVITES, write out an invitation normally, then tape it to a window with the writing side facing out. Place a sheet of coloured paper against the window and over the invite, and trace the words. You will have traced an invitation that can only be read in a looking glass. Complete your invites by decorating them with playing cards from the hearts suit, or with paintings of characters from *Alice in Wonderland*. You could also attach reflective silver card or a small mirror.

PARTY PHOTOGRAPHS

MAKE OR HIRE A LARGE GILT FRAME, or paint a backdrop of Alice playing croquet with the Queen of Hearts. Set this up in the entrance to the venue, and ask guests to pose for Polaroids as they arrive, either in front of the backdrop or behind the frame. Present the pictures to guests on leaving, or mount them in a photo album, and ask guests to sign beneath.

SHIMMY PARTY

RECREATE THE DAYS OF *THE GREAT GATSBY*, AND SPEND AN EVENING DANCING THE CHARLESTON.

Costumes Women in flapper dresses covered in sequins and bugle beads, and wearing silk stockings and garters, ostrich plumes, swinging beads and boyish hair. Men in smart evening suits, dress-shirts and bow ties or cravats.

Decor Art Deco: trim curtains with bullion fringing and stand peacock feathers and ostrich plumes in elegant vases. Fill the room with ferns placed on tall pedestals.

Table For a decadent air, make banknote napkin holders and coasters out of children's money (*see left*). Light the table with oyster candles. Melt small white candles in a tin can over a low heat. When melted, remove the wicks and cut into short lengths. Pour some wax into cleaned oyster-shell halves, and stand a wick in the centre of each. Hold the wicks upright for 30 seconds, until the wax sets.

Entertainment Dress waiting staff as famous silent movie stars such as Rudolph Valentino and Greta Garbo.

MYTHOLOGY BANQUET

DRESS AS ANCIENT GODS, AND ENJOY A NIGHT OF GOOD FOOD, FINE WINE AND MERRY-MAKING.

Invite Drawn to resemble sets of pan pipes.

Costumes Dress as the Minotaur, Pluto, Zeus, Andromeda, Agamemnon, Cyclops, Hercules, Atlas, Jason or Medusa.

Decor Hang up oil-burning lamps and stand terracotta urns and fake grape vines around the room. Make statue heads out of papier-mâché, paint them white and crown them with gold-sprayed laurel leaf crowns (*see right*).

Food Cover platters with vine leaves and serve herby garlic olives (*see page 89*), chargrilled chicken with figs (*see page 99*) festive filo pie (*see page 107*), honey cakes, poached peaches (*see page 111*), fresh cheeses, grapes, fruit and nuts and baskets of breads. Serve wine from terracotta urns or brass jugs.

Entertainment Dress serving staff as slaves. Seat a harpist at the door to welcome guests, and hire musicians to play the lyre and the pipes for guests to dance to. Hire actors to dress as a poet, a wandering philosopher and living statues.

WINTER WEDDING

BREAK WITH TRADITION AND GIVE AN ELIZABETHAN FEEL TO A WINTER WEDDING, USING LUXURIOUS VELVETS, BROCADES AND FAUX FURS.

Spray candlesticks gold, and fit them with long tapers. Wrap trailing ivy around the candlesticks and stick individual ivy leaves to each taper.

△ INVITES & DECORATIONS

FORAGE IN HEDGEROWS FOR BERRIES, LEAVES, PINECONES AND EVERGREENS TO DECORATE THE VENUE AND TABLES, SO THAT EVERYTHING LOOKS AND SMELLS WONDERFUL.

Invite Match to designs on the bride's gown, emboss in gold and send in gold envelopes sealed with sealing wax.

Decor Scatter herbs on the entrance floor, so when guests arrive, the air is filled with fragrance. Ideal herbs are thyme, mint and lemon balm. Hang up wreaths of evergreens, garnet-coloured roses and cinnamon (*see above*), and hand out buttonholes of winter berries. Secure swags of evergreen and pine cones tied with gold ribbon (*see page 42*) under windows.

THE RECEPTION ▷

Music Hire a musician to play music on the mandolin.

Table To make cinnamon candles, stretch elastic bands around church candles. Tuck cinnamon sticks of the same length under the bands, tie ribbons around and remove the bands (*see right*). Enjoy the wedding meal by candlelight.

Food Serve treacle glazed ham (*see page 102*), pommes dauphinoises (*see page 106*) and roast yams (*see page 107*). Finish with a cheese platter, served with figs and dates.

Drinks Hot toddies on arrival.

Bouquet Hand-tied roses wrapped in evergreens.

COUNTRY WEDDING

A COUNTRY THEME WORKS WELL FOR A SUMMER WEDDING. KEEP THE COLOURS SOFT AND FEMININE, AND MAKE THE MOST OF THE ABUNDANCE OF FLOWERS.

THE MEANING OF FLOWERS

Bluebell – everlasting love ★ Daffodil – regard
Daisy – innocence ★ Honeysuckle – devoted affection
Ivy – fidelity ★ White rose – worthiness
Myrtle – love ★ Orchid – beauty ★ Rose – romance
Violet – faithfulness ★ Lily of the valley – happiness
Red chrysanthemum – I love you ★ Tuberose – voluptuousness
Forget-me-not – remembrance always ★ Mimosa – secret love
Camellia – perfect loveliness ★ Hyacinth – playfulness

△ INVITES & DECORATIONS ▽

HAND OUT ORGANZA POUCHES OF LOOSE WHEAT SEEDS AND PETALS FOR GUESTS TO THROW AS CONFETTI.

Invite Stamp two gold hearts on heavy card. Attach two wheat ears, a sign of fertility, to each card (see above).

Decor Gather wild flowers, such as chamomile, buttercups and cornflowers and mix them with shop-bought hebes, lisianthus and spray roses. Arrange the flowers in silver tin cans tied with co-ordinated ribbon and set them around the wedding venue (see below). Use wide ribbons cut from the bridesmaids' dress fabric to tie bunches of wheat, and attach them over the entrance to form an archway.

THE RECEPTION

Music Hire a Celtic ceilidh or barn-dance band.

Table Cover tables in pastel-coloured linen, with each laid in a different colour. Tie napkins with woven wheat stems.

Food To continue the informal theme, host a country barbecue or eat in the garden, buffet style.

Drinks Bucks Fizz (see page 90) on arrival.

Bouquet Wheat ears, lavender, wild roses and rosebuds, elderflowers, honeysuckle, cornflowers or sweet peas, hand-tied with co-ordinated ribbons. Wear circlets of flowers and give bridesmaids small baskets of loose flowers to carry.

PETAL CONFETTI ▽

ROSE CONFETTI (*see below*) smells wonderful. Pick roses on the wedding morning. Pull off petals and put with rose heads in silk, velvet or organza bags. To make the bags, cut out fabric twice the size of the final bag. Fold in half, right sides facing, stitch the sides together, and turn out. Cut a flap shape, zigzag stitch the edges, and stitch to the front of the bag. Attach a tag and fill with petals.

UNUSUAL WEDDING VENUES

Castle ★ Yacht ★ Train
Hunting lodge ★ Barge ★ Clipper
Zoo ★ Restaurant ★ Stately home
Pub ★ Hotel ★ On the piste
Island ★ Chapel of Love, Las Vegas
Aeroplane ★ Garden
Under water ★ Hot-air balloon
Football stadium ★ On stage
Parachuting ★ Bungee jumping
By a lake ★ Up a mountain
Film set ★ Empire State Building

SILK RING CUSHION

MAKE A BEAUTIFUL white silk cushion edged with lace and embroidered with the names of the bride and groom, the date of the wedding and decorated with hearts, flowers or doves. Stitch two ribbons to the front and tie the wedding rings to them with a bow. A page boy could follow the bridal party up the aisle carrying the cushion, and present it to the best man when the rings are called for.

ORGANZA POUCHES

AT SUMMER WEDDINGS, instead of giving favours, make delicate pouches from organza and place wild flower seeds inside. The seeds can be sown in guests' gardens or window boxes to flower around your first wedding anniversary. To make the pouches, simply place a handful of seeds in the centre of a white circle of organza, scoop up the sides to make a purse shape and tie with a lavender-coloured ribbon.

WINTER CAKE TABLE

FOR A SETTING that perfectly complements a winter wedding cake, cover a small, round table with a round cloth. Set the cake on a cake stand in the centre. Swathe several metres of white tulle around the cake, covering the stand and tucking it under the cake board to resemble billowing snow. Scatter the tulle with cones, holly, mistletoe and white roses.

AUTUMN INVITATION

COMMISSION an illustration of the church or venue and print on card. Punch two holes down the side of each, and thread with a wheat ear.

WHEAT BUNCHES

GATHER BUNCHES of oats, wheat or corn and strip off the leaves. Take 40 stems and tie below the ears. Plant in terracotta pots filled with florists' foam and cover each pot with moss.

ROSE PLACE SETTING

LIGHTLY SPRAY tiny terracotta pots with gold or silver paint. Fill them with florist's foam and cover the top of each with moss. Trim the stems of dried roses to 10cm (4in) in length and stand a rose in the centre of each pot. Attach a parcel label to each, with wedding guests' names hand-written on them, and use the pots as place settings on the wedding reception tables.

WHITE WEDDING

STICK WITH TRADITION but give your white wedding a contemporary twist. Introduce a theme such as daisies, stars, feathers, candles, fake fur, snowflakes or cherubs to tie in with the time of year. Send out white invitations featuring your theme, such as a threaded feather or stuck-on stars or daisies. Ask guests to dress from head to foot in white and to wear a white buttonhole.

GOLDEN CHAIRS

TRANSFORM plain wooden chairs by brightening them up with a coat of paint. Sand down the chairs, ensure they are completely dust-free, then spray with gold paint.

TULLE CHAIRS

FOR A ROMANTIC TOUCH, tie white tulle bows to each chair. Cut lengths of tulle 50 x 150cm (20 x 60in) long. Wrap one around each chair back and secure at the back with a bow.

OUTDOOR LIGHTS

GLAM UP outdoor fairylights by placing a white greaseproof-paper bag over each bulb and securing it with a mini bulldog clip. Alternatively, make small, coloured paper envelopes for each light from different coloured tissue paper. Punch two holes in each envelope, thread with thin wire and use to secure the bag over each light.

MODERN WEDDING

HAVE A TAILOR-MADE wedding of your dreams. Choose a colour theme and inject a riot of colour into the ceremony, specify a costume theme or dress in outfits from the 1950s or 1960s, or as the characters from a favourite film. Set the tone for the day by arriving in a convertible car or a Cadillac, and ask ushers to hand out pots of bubbles to guests, so that you emerge from the wedding ceremony in a cloud of bubbles.

MODERN WEDDING RECEPTION

SPREAD TABLES with a white cloth and overlay them with another cloth in a bright, translucent colour. Wire name tags, push each one into a fresh lemon and stand it on a plate as a place setting. When guests arrive, offer them a cocktail such as a margarita or banana daiquiri (*see page 90*). Serve informal food that is a favourite with the bride and groom, such as sausages and mash, pasta, sushi or tacos.

MODERN WEDDING DECOR

WIRE BAY TREES with oranges and lemons, and stand them at the entrance to the venue. Give out button holes made with gerberas, and decorate the venue with bunches of sunflowers or anemones in coloured glass bottles and jars. Light the outside area with flaming torches or petal flares (*see page 19*).

Fill shallow glass △ bowls with flowers and pebbles, and float candles around the edges.

HALLOWE'EN, THANKSGIVING, CHRISTMAS, NEW YEAR'S EVE – THE FESTIVE SEASON IS THE TIME TO THROW A PARTY. STICK TO THE BARE ESSENTIALS TRADITIONAL TO THE OCCASION, OR GO ALL OUT FOR AN OVER-THE-TOP CELEBRATION WITH SHIMMERING SEASONAL DECORATIONS AND ATMOSPHERIC FOOD AND DRINK.

FESTIVE PARTIES

ON CHRISTMAS DAY SHARE THE PREPARATION AND COST OF A MEAL BY ENJOYING A HOUSE-HOPPING, MENU-SHARING CHRISTMAS DINNER WITH NEARBY FRIENDS AND FAMILY. HOLD A TREASURE HUNT FOR CHILDREN, WITH CLUES LEADING FROM ONE HOUSE TO THE NEXT, AND EAT A DIFFERENT COURSE AT EACH HOUSE, STARTING WITH A BRUNCH OF SMOKED SALMON AND CHAMPAGNE.

HALLOWE'EN

FOR A NIGHT OF FIENDISH FUN, SEND INVITATIONS IN BLACK ENVELOPES STAMPED WITH BLOOD-RED SEALING WAX, CARVE SPOOKY FACES IN PUMPKINS, AND SERVE GUESTS BAT BISCUITS AND WORM SOUP.

WITCHES' PARTY

▽

PIN UP SCARY ORGANZA GHOST SHAPES FROM CEILINGS TO BRUSH AGAINST GUESTS' FACES.

Invite Mail out jelly worms, spiders and bats (*see below*).

Costumes Witches, black cats, warlocks, goblins and trolls.

Decor Stand pumpkin lanterns (*see below*) at the entrance.

Food Worm soup made with thick noodles, bat-shaped gingerbread biscuits (*see page 114*), toffee apples, pumpkin pie.

Games Face painting, apple bobbing, ghost stories. Hide trick-or-treat party bags outdoors, under piles of raked leaves.

HORROR PARTY

USE THE HORROR FILMS OF BORIS KARLOFF, VINCENT PRICE AND PETER CUSHING AS INSPIRATION.

Costumes Dress as zombies, or whiten your face, grease back your hair, don a cape and come as Dracula.

Decor Create a dungeon by hanging chains from the ceiling, burning red-hot coals in the grate and lighting the room with candles in red-painted glass jars. Run classic black-and-white horror movies on the video.

Music *Thriller* by Michael Jackson; demented organ playing.

Games Murder in the dark, sardines (*see page 47*), Cluedo.

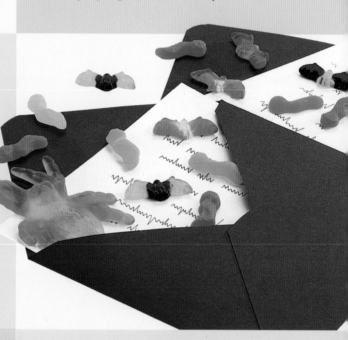

CARVED PUMPKIN LIGHTING

CLEVERLY CARVED PUMPKINS make scary but fun lanterns for Hallowe'en parties. Cut the top off a pumpkin or squash, and scoop out the flesh as neatly as possible. Draw outlines of eyes, nose and a jagged mouth on the pumpkin with a marker pen (*see right*). Using a craft knife or scalpel, carefully carve around the outlines, then cut through the skin and flesh. Remove the carved-out pieces of pumpkin, taking care not to split the skin and flesh around the cut-out shapes. Set a night-light or candles inside.

HALLOWE'EN MENU

CREAMY PUMPKIN SOUP (*SEE PAGE 92*)

•

BEEF IN BEER, SERVED FROM A BOWL INSIDE A HOLLOWED-OUT PUMPKIN (*SEE PAGE 98*)

CHEESY JACKET POTATOES (*SEE PAGE 106*)

•

GHOST-SHAPED MERINGUE GATEAU (*SEE PAGE 108*)

•

WITCH'S BREW (LEMONADE WITH GREEN FOOD COLOURING), APPLE WHIZZ AND MULLED WINE (*SEE PAGE 91*)

FIREWORKS

ENJOY AN EVENING OF FURIOUS FLAMES AND FIREWORKS. HANG UP LUMINOUS STARS, STAND SPARKLERS IN POTS OF SAND, BURY POTATOES IN THE FIRE'S EMBERS, AND TOAST MOUNDS OF MARSHMALLOWS.

FIREWORKS MENU

ROASTED PEPPER & TOMATO SOUP (*SEE PAGE 92*)

•

CHILLI CON CARNE

POTATOES, BAKED IN EMBERS (*SEE PAGE 24*)

•

BAKED APPLES

BONFIRE CAKES (*SEE PAGE 114*)

OVERSIZED TRIPLE CHOC COOKIES (*SEE PAGE 116*), SERVED IN GREASEPROOF BAGS

STARGAZER'S PARTY

THROW A NIGHT-TIME PARTY OF SHOOTING STARS, PLANETS AND CONSTELLATIONS. ASK GUESTS TO BRING TELESCOPES AND BINOCULARS, AND HAND OUT ASTRAL MAPS.

Invite Send packets of sparkling moondust and invite guests to come dressed as gods, or as their sign of the zodiac.

Costumes Zeus, Thor, Eros, Libra, Capricorn, Virgo and Aries.

Decor Hang fairy lights in trees and dot petal flares around the garden (*see page 19*). Spray chairs gold for the gods' feast.

Music *The Planets* by Gustav Holst.

Entertainment Finish the night with dazzling fireworks.

FIREWORKS PARTY

FOR A REALLY SPECTACULAR SHOW, ASK EACH GUEST TO DONATE A SET AMOUNT TO THE FIREWORK FUND, AND START COLLECTING FIREWOOD A FEW WEEKS IN ADVANCE.

Invite Attach labels to packs of liquorice Catherine wheels.

Decor Illuminate the garden by punching designs in tin cans and setting night-lights inside (*see below*).

Food Mashed potato spiked with sausages, bananas baked with chocolate (*see page 24*), toasted marshmallows.

Drinks Hot chocolate, mulled wine (*see page 90*), Swedish Glogg (*see page 43*), Irish coffee (*see page 13*) and spiced cider.

FIREWORKS DECOR ▷

★ Tin-can lights make decorative, safe candle holders. Clean a tin can with paint stripper and wire wool. Cut the top off the can with strong scissors, then cut a decorative shape around the front and back, and discard the surplus metal. Keep the design at least 3cm (1½in) high at the base. Punch a design on the can using a bradawl or a hammer and nail. Set a candle inside.

★ For a lovely table setting, pick brilliantly coloured red, orange and green leaves. Lay the leaves between blotting paper and press overnight. Overlay three leaves around the base of a red candle, leaving a space below for the candle to fit in the holder. Overlap more leaves to resemble petals, and secure with raffia.

THANKSGIVING

CELEBRATE ON THE FOURTH THURSDAY IN NOVEMBER BY GATHERING FAMILY AND FRIENDS TO GIVE THANKS FOR THE GOOD THINGS IN LIFE. TO TRANSFORM A TABLECLOTH FOR THANKSGIVING DINNER, PAINT THE VEINED SIDES OF PRESSED LEAVES WITH FABRIC PAINT AND STAMP ON TO THE CLOTH. FIX THE DRIED DESIGN WITH AN IRON.

THANKSGIVING DINNER

FOR PLACE SETTINGS, PAINT THE VEINED SIDE OF DRIED, PRESSED LEAVES WITH EMULSION OR POSTER PAINT AND STAMP ON TO RECTANGLES OF WHITE CARD. WHEN DRY, CUT AROUND HALF THE PRINT, FOLD THE CARD IN TWO AND WRITE ON THE NAME (*SEE ABOVE*).

Decor Print a leaf tablecloth and place settings (*see above*). Give the tablecloth variety by printing it with as many different leaves as possible. Make a cornucopia centrepiece for the table by wrapping and taping card around a cone-shaped piece of florist's foam. Remove the foam, and cover the card with papier-mâché strips made from newspaper and wallpaper paste; give three coats inside and out. When dry, paint the cone and seal it with two coats of satin varnish. Place the cornucopia on a table and fill with a cascade of attractive fruits.

Food Serve roast turkey garnished with halved clementine shells filled with blueberries and cranberries.

Entertainment Everyone play charades in the evening.

THANKSGIVING MENU

CORNBREAD (*SEE PAGE 88*)

CREAMY PUMPKIN SOUP (*SEE PAGE 92*)
•
BONED STUFFED TURKEY (*SEE PAGE 103*)

ROAST SWEET POTATOES (*SEE PAGE 107*)

COURGETTES WITH GARLIC (*SEE PAGE 107*)

ROAST, BUTTERED PUMPKIN

WILD RICE
•
INDIVIDUAL PECAN PIES
(*SEE PAGE 112*)

CHRISTMAS

DON'T LET A LACK OF SPACE STOP YOU DECORATING A TREE THIS CHRISTMAS: SELECT BRANCHES OF TWISTED WILLOW, AND FROST WITH SILVER SPRAY PAINT. PUSH THE BRANCHES INTO A VASE OF FLORIST'S FOAM, AND HANG WITH BAUBLES AND BOWS. SEND OUT GINGERBREAD HEARTS, ICED AND WRAPPED IN CELLOPHANE, INSTEAD OF CHRISTMAS CARDS.

MIDNIGHT MASS

CHILDREN NEVER SLEEP ON CHRISTMAS EVE, SO LET THEM STAY UP AND JOIN YOU AT EVENING MASS.

Invite Send out invites with Christmas cards, asking each child to bring a glass jar and a night-light.

Food Enlist the children's help in baking triple choc cookies (*see page 116*) for Santa, using shaped cookie cutters.

Drinks Hot chocolate and, for the adults, mulled wine (*see page 91*) and Irish coffee (*see Hot Toddies, page 13*).

Entertainment Spend the evening writing Santa letters and decorating the glass jars with glass paints and sticky shapes. To make jar handles, loop a long piece of string into a handle, then wrap the rest of the string around the jar rim, tying the ends in a knot. Leave the cookies and a drink out for Santa, then light the jar lanterns and walk to church singing Christmas carols. Surprise the children on their return: sneak home while everyone is at church, take a bite out of a cookie, finish the drink, make hoof prints in the snow and hang up a stocking for each child.

SWEDISH CHRISTMAS ▷

ENJOY A SWEDISH *JULBORD*, THE PERFECT MEAL TO SERVE FOR AN "OPEN HOUSE" CHRISTMAS. TELL GUESTS TO DROP IN AT THEIR LEISURE AND JOIN YOU FOR A BITE TO EAT, A GAME OR TWO, AND A GLASS OF GLOGG.

Invite Pipe on to gingerbread (*see page 114*).

Decor Stand traditional Swedish candles in every window. Decorate a tree with gingerbread biscuits (*see right*). To make these, cut gingerbread dough (*see page 114*) into star, heart and tree shapes. Punch holes in the top for ribbon, bake, then ice, thread with ribbon and hang on the tree.

Food Translated, *Julbord* simply means "Christmas table", so emulate a Swedish Christmas and offer an extensive buffet. Serve roast ham, mustard, pickled cabbage and apple sauce, rolled herrings and gravadlax, meatballs, pâté, cold meats, sausages and gingerbread biscuits called *pepparkakor*.

Drinks Serve steaming cups of Glogg (*see page 43*), made from red wine, vodka and spices.

TWIG FIR TREE

MAKE A FIR-TREE shape from stiff wire. Paint a clay pot, stand the tree trunk in it, pour in plaster of Paris and, when set, cover with moss. Attach bundles of twigs to the tree with wire. Thread cranberries on to cotton thread, and zigzag it up the tree, securing with wire at intervals. Attach dried orange slices (*see page 44*), rag bows, baubles and holly as a star (*see right*).

PINE CONE BUNDLES

THESE BUNDLES MAKE ATTRACTIVE, SCENTED CHRISTMAS DECORATIONS.

Place pine cones on a tray and leave to dry and open in an airing cupboard or warm, dry place. Dot glue on to each scale, then sprinkle with glitter. Glue a long length of ribbon to the base of each cone, then gather ten cones and tie the ribbons into a bow. Attach a bundle to either end of a shelf and sprinkle the cones with a little pine oil.

Tiny Christmas cakes baked in tin cans make lovely gifts. Ice them, then wrap in cellophane.

LUMINARY

THIS LANTERN GIVES A ROOM A WONDERFUL CHRISTMAS FEEL.

Cut a rectangle of coloured thick or corrugated cardboard to measure 20 x 61cm (8 x 24in). Score a line every 15cm (6in) down the long edge of the card. Cut a Christmas shape, such as a star, angel or holly out of each quarter. Glue greaseproof paper behind each shape, then fold and stand the luminary over a night-light.

OAK LEAF RUNNER

FOR A QUICK decoration to run the length of a table, take a strip of corded ribbon about 5cm (2in) wide and at least 1m (40in) longer than the table. Cut "V" shapes at both ends of the ribbon. Glue a small pine cone to the ribbon at both ends of the table, then glue large, dried oak leaves along the length of the ribbon.

CHILLI WREATH

THREAD RED AND GREEN chillies on lengths of string, and hang in a warm, dry place, such as an airing cupboard, to dry out and harden. When they are dry, glue the chillies around a simple cane wreath, following the weave of the wreath. When the wreath is covered, tie with ribbon and hang up.

YULE LOG

USE A YULE LOG as a centrepiece. Find a stout, gnarled silver birch or apple tree log. Put the log on a flat surface, so it sits squarely, and drill seven 2cm (¾in) deep by 2cm (¾in) wide holes evenly along the top. Stand a candle in each hole and decorate with holly.

SNOWFLAKE SCENE

DRAW A SIX-POINTED snowflake shape onto a sheet of medium-weight cardboard. Cut out the shape on the card, using a craft knife or scalpel. Hold the card template firmly against the inside of a clean window, and lightly spray through the shape, using fake aerosol snow. Carefully remove the stencil and repeat randomly over the windows to form a snowy scene.

CHRISTMAS MENU

SMOKED SALMON TRIANGLES
(SEE PAGE 95)

•

BONED STUFFED TURKEY
(SEE PAGE 103)

POMMES DAUPHINOIS
(SEE PAGE 106)

ROAST PARSNIPS

•

PLUM PUDDING (SEE PAGE 110)

PAPER CHAINS

PAPER CHAINS ARE SIMPLE TO MAKE, AND CHILDREN CAN HELP.

Cut two long strips of coloured paper, each about 5cm (2in) wide. Lay one end of each strip at right angles to the other and staple the ends in place. Fold one strip over the other at right angles, and crease the fold. Repeat, folding the strips alternately over each other until the paper is used up, then staple the ends together.

FIRE & ICE PARTY

IF CELEBRATING CHRISTMAS IN SNOWY CLIMES, THROW A CHILDREN'S PARTY.

Ask children to bring gloves, hats and a tea tray or toboggan. Hold sledge races, then warm up with hot chocolate, with marshmallows floating on top. Divide children into groups and ask each group to build the best snowman. Enjoy an ice cream birthday cake and hand out sparklers to illuminate the way home.

For a glittering Christmas tree, deck branches in white, frosted glass and shimmering silver.

LUCKY-DIP PARTY

ASK GUESTS TO BRING LUCKY-DIP GIFTS TO A SET VALUE.

Fill a box with shredded paper and bury the gifts as guests arrive. After supper, take turns to pick a gift. If you know your guests very well, it can be more fun to buy anonymous presents for specific friends. Put guests' names in a hat, draw them out and enclose in the invitations.

SWEDISH GLOGG

PUT A FEW PLUMP raisins and blanched almonds in the base of six glasses. Pour a bottle of red wine into a pan. Add 150ml (¼pt) vodka, 5 cloves, 2 cinnamon sticks, 8 cardamom pods and sugar to taste. Bring almost to the boil, remove from the heat, strain, then pour into glasses. Let the glogg stand overnight in the pan for a stronger drink.

CHRISTMAS SWAGS

HANG DECORATIVE DRIED FRUIT SWAGS FROM FIREPLACES, ALONG SHELVES AND DOWN BANNISTERS.

Thinly slice oranges and lemons into 5mm (⅛in) slices and place them on wire racks set over baking sheets. Bake at 140°C/275°F/Gas 1 for 7–8 hours with the oven door ajar, until the slices have dried and are no longer sticky. Check the slices at intervals, as drying time can vary greatly. Remove the fruit from the oven and let it cool. Thread the slices alternately with dried cranberries, bay leaves, small wooden hearts, whole dried pomegranates and rag ribbon bows, on to long lengths of jute string, and hang up.

For original, glittering place settings, spell out guests' initials using gold- and silver-coloured sugared almonds or dragées.

△ SILVER & GOLD PARTY

Costumes This colour theme is one that even the most reluctant fancy-dress party guest can join in with, whether guests dress from head to toe in silver and gold, or simply don one item of coloured clothing or glitter make-up.

Decor Sand down old wooden chairs, then spray them with gold paint. Transform cheap glasses with swirls of gold and silver relief paint (*see page 28*). Tie linen napkins with thick gold braid.

Food Gild food with edible loose-leaf gold, and cover cakes or ice cream with tiny silver dragées.

HOME-MADE CRACKERS

BUY CRACKER SNAPS if possible, so the crackers bang when pulled. Cut three rectangles of card 13 x 11cm (5 x 4½in), and roll into three tubes, securing each with tape. Place a snap in one tube, to hang evenly from both ends, then stuff a small gift, a silly joke and a party hat inside. Glue the tube halfway down the long edge of a 32 x 25cm (13 x 10in) rectangle of crêpe paper. Lay the two other tubes at both ends of the glued tube, leaving a 3cm (1¼in) gap between them. Wrap the crêpe paper around the tubes and glue in place. Tie gold string into tight bows in the gaps between the rolls. Remove the end rolls and decorate.

New Year's Eve

GATHER WITH FRIENDS TO SEE IN THE NEW YEAR. HAND OUT BELLS AND HOOTERS, AND MAKE AS MUCH NOISE AS POSSIBLE AT MIDNIGHT!

Scottish New Year's Eve

GREET THE NEW YEAR IN TRUE SCOTTISH STYLE.

Invite Tie invitations with a tartan ribbon, and ask guests to dress in kilts and tartan.

Drinks Float aromatic clove-studded orange slices in glasses of mulled wine (*see page 91*).

Entertainment Light up the garden with flaming torches, and treat guests to a firework display. Dance the evening away to Scottish reels before turning up the radio and handing out whistles and bells to sound in the new year. Welcome in the new year by singing "auld lang syne", then go first-footing (*see left*).

First-footing

JUST AFTER MIDNIGHT, throw open your front door and "first-foot" to your neighbour's home. Take a gift, as arriving empty-handed brings bad luck; gifts often include coal, bread, salt or whisky. If first-footers arrive at your home, welcome them with whisky and shortbread to ensure a happy new year.

Tartan Trimmings

BRIGHTEN UP plain napkins and tablecloths by adding a tartan trim. Sew wide lengths of colourful tartan ribbon on to the edges of the fabric to form a border. Continue the tartan theme by painting a terracotta pot with a bright tartan design, then plant it with heather or a flowering pot plant.

Shortbread Boxes ▷

OFFER TARTAN BOXES OF SHORTBREAD TO FIRST-FOOTERS OR DEPARTING GUESTS. TRADITIONALLY, THE SHORTBREAD IS SHAPED IN "PETTICOAT TAILS".

Paint a box a bright colour with poster or emulsion paint. Glue a length of tartan ribbon around the edge of the box lid, gluing any excess width of ribbon inside the box. To make a rosette, loop another length of tartan ribbon eight times, gluing it in place each time it crosses the centre. Add dried heather, lavender or artificial flowers, sticking them in place between the rosette loops, and glue the rosette to the box. Line the box with tissue paper and fill with shortbread.

For a potentially prosperous new year, enclose a lottery ticket in new year cards.

CANDLE TABLE SETTING

CREATE A DRAMATIC CENTREPIECE for a New Year's Eve dinner or buffet table. Fill a shallow glass bowl with water and float green scented candles on the surface. Stand small, fat church candles and little pot plants set with tapers alternately around the edge of the bowl. Surround the candles with a ring of flat pebbles. Light the candles and enjoy.

SPANISH NEW YEAR

A SPANISH FIESTA is a great way to see in the new year. Drink cava and serve tortilla, paella, and prawns, crabs and oysters on an ice tray (*see page 78*). Give each guest twelve grapes just before midnight. The tradition is to try to eat a grape on each chime of midnight; the number of grapes a person manages to eat is said to bring good luck for that many months of the new year.

NEW YEAR'S EVE MENU

ASPARAGUS AND LIME PASTA
(*SEE PAGE 94*)

•

BOEUF EN CROÛTE (*SEE PAGE 102*)

FESTIVE FILO PIE (*SEE PAGE 107*)

CARROT AND COURGETTE MEDLEY

•

MINCEMEAT CHRISTMAS BOMBE
(*SEE PAGE 110*)

CHINESE NEW YEAR

CELEBRATE NEW YEAR in Chinese style, for a party with a splash of bright colour. Attach invitations to fortune cookies or Chinese good-luck calendars and sign off with "*Kung Hei Fat Choy*", which means "we hope you get rich". Decorate the venue in reds, purples and gold, and hang up delicate paper lanterns (*see right*). Serve up a banquet of Chinese delicacies and set off firecrackers at midnight.

ORIENTAL LANTERNS ▷

CUT GOLD CARD 65 x 20cm (25½ x 8in) wide. Measure 2.5cm (1in) in from one of the short ends and mark with a line. Mark three more lines at 15cm (6in) intervals. Draw a 1.5cm (½in) frame in each of the four equal sections and cut out the centre of each with a craft knife. Stick tissue or newspaper inside each panel and glue a tassel on each corner. Fold the card at the marked lines and glue the long tab to the furthest panel, to make a square. Hang up with wire.

PARTY GAMES

GAMES HELP TO BREAK
THE ICE BETWEEN GUESTS;
DON'T FORGET TO BUY
PRIZES FOR THE WINNERS.

TABOO

PICK A WORD that often comes up in conversation, such as "yes", "no", "and" or "I", and make it taboo. Choose one guest to be questioned by the others in turn, who try to make them say the taboo word. The object of the game is for the chosen guest to last a full minute without being caught out or hesitating. This is not as easy as it seems.

SARDINES

NAME SOMEONE AS "IT" and ask everyone else to count to 100 while the chosen person hides. Guests set off to find "it"; when someone does so, they too hide in the same place. This becomes harder as more and more guests find the hiding place. The object of the game is to squeeze everyone into the same space without alerting those still looking. Warn guests not to hide in a bath – they are not strong enough for more than three people!

MUSICAL CUSHIONS

PLAY THIS GAME as you would musical chairs, but using cushions. Guests dance to music around a line of cushions. When it stops, each must dive on to a cushion. Whoever does not get a cushion is out. Continue until there is a winner. The advantage of musical cushions over musical chairs is that guests can not break or fall off a cushion.

ASSOCIATIONS

INVITE A GUEST to say the first word that comes into their head. A second guest must rapidly answer with a word somehow associated with the first word. The word chain continues around the group until someone breaks the chain by saying a word that isn't closely enough associated with the previous word. That guest drops out, and a new game begins, starting with a new word. Play until there is a winner.

PASS THE BOTTLE

DIVIDE GUESTS into two teams, standing in two lines. The players at the front begin with a bottle clenched between their knees. This should be passed to the knees of the next team member without being touched by any hands. If someone drops the bottle, they must retrieve it with their knees. The first team to pass the bottle along the whole line wins.

FOR AN EXTRA-SPECIAL BIRTHDAY, WEDDING ANNIVERSARY OR FAMILY CELEBRATION, CHOOSE A SPECTACULAR SETTING. INVENTIVE VENUES FOR PARTIES RANGE FROM A SNOWY SKI LODGE OR SUN-BAKED VINEYARD TO AN ANCIENT CASTLE OR STATELY HOME. AN AWE-INSPIRING NATURAL WONDER SUCH AS

SPECIAL OCCASIONS

A CAVE OR WATERFALL MAKES A CREATIVE SETTING, OR OPT FOR A MODERN MINIMALIST FEEL IN AN ICE RINK, ULTRA-CHIC ART GALLERY OR NIGHTCLUB. FOR THE ULTIMATE SPECIAL-OCCASION PARTY, PLAN AN OUT-OF-THIS-WORLD EXPERIENCE: HIRE A HOT-AIR BALLOON, TAKE TO THE SKIES ON A FERRIS WHEEL AT A FAIRGROUND, OR VIEW LIFE IN THE SEA FROM A GLASS-BOTTOMED BOAT.

BIRTHDAYS

BE IT AN 8TH OR AN 80TH BIRTHDAY PARTY, A LITTLE ORGANIZING IN ADVANCE CAN TRANSFORM THE OCCASION. NOT EVERYONE LOVES HUGE PARTIES, SO MATCH NUMBERS TO THE GUEST OF HONOUR'S PREFERENCE. DON'T FORGET TO PROVIDE PLENTY OF FINGER FOOD, AS WELL AS A DELICIOUS BIRTHDAY CAKE (SEE PAGES 116–17).

BLACK TIE 21ST PARTY

ON A SON'S OR DAUGHTER'S 21ST BIRTHDAY, HOLD A PARTY THEY WILL ALWAYS REMEMBER, AND INVITE THEIR FRIENDS TO DRESS UP FOR A BLACK–TIE EVENING.

Invite Incorporate a photograph of the host as a baby.

Decor Give the venue a sophisticated look with masses of black, white and silver balloons and streamers.

Table Use plain white tablecloths, and interweave wide strips of brightly coloured crêpe paper on top, to achieve a modern tartan effect. Use clashing colour combinations, such as orange and pink or lime green and red. Pile party poppers, streamers and string spray in the centre of each table.

Food Employ caterers and treat guests to a silver service three-course meal.

Entertainment Find a stand-up comedian to perform while guests eat. After the meal, set aside a separate room for older guests to adjourn to, so younger guests can enjoy themselves to the full with a hired disco or band.

OSCAR NIGHT ▷

INVITE FRIENDS TO A NIGHT AT THE OSCARS. THEME EACH TABLE TO A DIFFERENT FILM, AND ASK GUESTS TO DRESS AS THE CHARACTERS.

Costumes Guests could dress as characters from films such as: *The Thief of Bagdad, Barbarella, Ben Hur, La Dolce Vita, Cabaret, Some Like It Hot, The Magnificent Seven, My Fair Lady, Saturday Night Fever, Cyrano de Bergerac, Star Wars, Titanic.*

Decor Model a huge papier-mâché Oscar to stand at the entrance. Cut five-pointed star shapes from sheets of card, and use them as stencils to spray cascades of gold and silver stars on tablecloths (*see right*). Hang stars and a glitter ball from the ceiling, and set up moving spotlights.

Drinks Build a champagne fountain to greet guests on arrival. Have a cocktail barman mixing cocktails to order.

Entertainment Take each guest's photograph next to the Oscar. Place silver-sprayed disposable cameras on tables (*see right*). Hire a band to play film scores, or Fred Astaire and Ginger Rogers lookalikes to start the dancing.

Enjoy a day of mystery and suspense with a murder-mystery party on a train. Ask guests to dress in 1920s-style clothing, and book a jazz band to accompany the journey.

ORIENT EXPRESS BIRTHDAY

HIRE A RESTORED STEAM TRAIN FOR A SPECIAL BIRTHDAY CELEBRATION, AND RELIVE THE HEYDAY OF THE 1920s AND AGATHA CHRISTIE.

Invite Print invitations to look like railway tickets.

Costumes Adopt period costume, with women in flapper dresses and feather boas, and men in lounge suits. Dress catering staff in Twenties-style butler and maid costumes.

Music Hire a jazz band to welcome guests aboard.

Food Serve delicious canapés, such as salmon pinwheels (*see page 86*), cheese twists (*see page 88*) and blini with quail's eggs and smoked fish (*see page 89*).

Entertainment Host a murder-mystery game, with friends playing different roles, and spend an afternoon in delicious suspense as you discover whodunnit.

LIFE BEGINS AT 40, 50 OR 60

WHEN A FRIEND OR FAMILY MEMBER HAS A MILESTONE-BIRTHDAY, BE SURE TO CELEBRATE IN STYLE.

Invite Secretly borrow the address book of your friend or relative, and list everyone who should be invited. Emphasize the need for secrecy on the invitations.

Decor Ask friends to help decorate the venue while others take the unsuspecting guest of honour out for the day. Collect a selection of photographs of the birthday guest, from childhood onwards. Enlarge them on a photocopier, paste to boards with captions and arrange around the venue.

Food Serve the guest of honour's favourite meal, whether it be pizza, hot dogs, or mounds of pastries and cakes.

Entertainment Invite guests to buy presents to help the guest of honour through the next ten years. Gifts could include a massage, golf lessons, a spa treatment, or a pedicure. Alternatively, several friends could buy a significant joint gift, such as a cruise, flying lessons, or a flight to a destination the birthday guest has always wanted to visit.

BACK TO SCHOOL PARTY

ENJOY AN EVENING OF NOISY TEENAGE NOSTALGIA, AS YOU AND YOUR FRIENDS GO BACK TO SCHOOL FOR THE NIGHT.

Costumes Dress as you did at school, complete with pigtails and school ties, scuffed shoes and yoyos.

Decor Ask guests to provide school-age photos of themselves in advance. Hang them on the wall and try to guess who is who.

Music Play the soundtrack to the movie *Grease*.

Table Cover table tops with sheets of MDF or plywood painted with blackboard paint. Chalk the dinner menu on the tables, and hand out chalks for guests to write messages and play wordgames with.

Food Serve dishes that are favourites with children. For dessert, bake a huge, iced birthday cake (*see page 117*).

Games Play rowdy games, such as musical cushions, associations and sardines (*see page 47*).

ORIENTAL BANQUET ▽

WHETHER YOU COOK YOUR OWN DISHES OR BUY FROM A LOCAL RESTAURANT, A BANQUET OF THAI OR CHINESE FOOD ALWAYS LOOKS STUNNING.

Invite Attach to a pair of wooden chopsticks.

Decor Arrange twisted willow, single stems of orchid, or bamboo in tall, elegant vases and set around the room. Gather a collection of smooth pebbles, and arrange in piles on empty surfaces.

Table Spread comfortable cushions on the floor around a low table. Cover the table with sheets from an Asian newspaper and place Bamboo Candles (*see right*) on top as a centrepiece. Lay out Orchid Napkins (*see right and below*) and serve food from bamboo steamers.

Food Complement the menu (*see right*) with rice bowls filled with prawn crackers and dishes of dipping sauces.

Drinks Serve jasmine tea, warm sake or plum wine in delicate Chinese tea cups.

BAMBOO CANDLES

A square glass vase makes an attractive vessel for this candle display. Cut lengths of green bamboo to the same height as the vase is deep. Tie around the outside of the vase with raffia, and fill the centre with tightly packed long white tapers.

ORCHID NAPKINS

Neatly roll up a white fabric napkin, then flatten it slightly. Fold a 20 x 30cm (8 x 12in) strip of newspaper in half lengthways, and wrap around the napkin, securing it with sticky tape. Tuck a pair of chopsticks beneath the paper strip, and place an orchid, jasmine flower or fortune cookie on top.

BANQUET MENU

SWEET & SOUR PRAWNS (*SEE PAGE 94*)

•

THAI GREEN CURRY (*SEE PAGE 103*)

STIR-FRIED GREEN VEGETABLES (*SEE PAGE 105*)

NOODLES

PLAIN BOILED THAI FRAGRANT RICE

•

COCONUT ICE CREAM (*SEE PAGE 113*)

MONEY-NO-OBJECT PRESENTS

Swimming with dolphins ★ *One day's falconry* ★ *Balloon flight*
Flying lesson ★ *Gliding lesson* ★ *Off-road driving*
Skiing lessons ★ *Vintage car racing* ★ *Trip to Victoria Falls*
Flight on Concorde ★ *Horse-riding lessons*
White-water rafting ★ *Health-club membership*
Waterskiing lessons ★ *Power boat racing* ★ *Record a song*
Lunch at the Eiffel Tower ★ *Scuba-diving lessons*
Golf lessons ★ *Clay-pigeon shooting* ★ *Whale watching*
Trip to New York ★ *Jet skiing* ★ *Salsa-dancing lessons*
Nile cruise ★ *Parachute jump*

ANNIVERSARIES

A PHOTOGRAPH ALBUM SHOWING A COUPLE'S YEARS TOGETHER MAKES A LOVELY GIFT. INTERVIEW FAMILY AND FRIENDS, AND ASK THEM TO SHARE THEIR MEMORIES BY DONATING A PHOTO FOR THE ALBUM.

To make a personalized plate ▷

for an anniversary couple,

ask guests to sign their names on

a platter using thermohardening

water-based ceramic paint.

WEDDING ANNIVERSARY THEMES

1st – paper ★ 2nd – cotton ★ 3rd – leather
4th – fruit and flowers ★ 5th – wood ★ 6th – sugar
7th – woollen ★ 8th – bronze ★ 9th – pottery
10th – tin ★ 12th – silk, fine linen ★ 15th – crystal
20th – china ★ 25th – silver ★ 30th – pearl
35th – coral ★ 40th – ruby ★ 50th – golden
55th – emerald ★ 60th – diamond
65th – blue sapphire ★ 70th – platinum

NIGHT OF NOSTALGIA

INVITE GUESTS to dress in clothing from the era you married in: 1940s' utility clothing; post-war New Look or demob suit; wide, flared skirts and leather jackets for the 1950s; hippy kaftans, beads and beards for the 1960s; disco sequins for the 1970s; and power dressing shoulder pads for the 1980s. Hire a disco or band to play the music that was popular in the year you married.

ANNIVERSARY AT THE RACES

HIRE A VINTAGE CAR and spend an anniversary at the races. Meet up with friends, and picnic on champagne before making your way to the race course and occupying a box for the day. Set up a sweepstake between guests by asking them to place a set sum in a hat. Ask everyone to pick winners for each race: award 10 points for a winner, five points for second place, and three points for third place. Whoever has the highest number of points at the end of the day takes the winnings.

THEME PARTIES

THROW A THEME PARTY TO MARK ANY OCCASION: A BAR MITZVAH, RETIREMENT, GRADUATION – OR JUST BECAUSE YOU WANT TO PARTY.

IDEAS FOR THEME PARTIES

The circus ★ Antarctica ★ Tintin
Highwaymen and outlaws ★ Angels
Victorian crinolines ★ The Addams Family
Sumo wrestlers and geisha girls ★ Batman
Saloon bar ★ Carmen Miranda
Shakespeare's plays ★ Aladdin ★ Dracula
Jaws ★ Imps and goblins ★ World leaders
Superman ★ Julius Caesar ★ Beauty and the Beast
Elvis ★ The Three Musketeers ★ Matadors
The Godfather ★ Mary Poppins

BEAUJOLAIS NOUVEAU PARTY

IN NOVEMBER, CELEBRATE THE ARRIVAL OF THE LATEST BEAUJOLAIS WINE WITH A PARTY.

Invite Send invitations out on mini French flags. Ask one-third of guests to dress in blue, one-third to dress in white and one-third to dress in red.

Music Play Edith Piaf, or Django Reinhardt's hot jazz.

Food Ask guests each to bring a portion of their favourite French cheese, while you supply bread, wine and grapes.

Entertainment Pit teams of different colours against each other in a series of races and games (*see page 47*).

COSTUME IDEAS FOR A GANGSTERS & MOLLS PARTY

TAKE INSPIRATION FROM *BONNIE AND CLYDE*, *BUGSY MALONE* AND JAMES CAGNEY FILMS.

Trilby hats ★ Cigarette holders ★ Sharp suits
Toy tommy-guns ★ Kohl-rimmed eyes ★ Spats
Black tie ★ Patent leather shoes ★ Large overcoats
Cloche hats ★ Dancer's feather costumes
Bobbed hair ★ Fake-fur wraps ★ Cupid-bow lips
Feather boas ★ Silk stockings ★ Sequins

PROHIBITION PARTY

RECREATE THE CHICAGO OF AL CAPONE AND THE PROHIBITION, WHEN GANGSTERS AND THEIR MOLLS HAUNTED NOTORIOUS SPEAKEASIES.

Costumes Dress in flapper dresses (*see left*), or as dancing girls in exotic costumes. Wear sharp suits and bring toy tommy-guns to complete the outfit.

Decor Keep the lighting low and intimate and black out the windows. Set up a bar area, run by a barman in braces.

Drinks Serve bourbon as "hooch". Ask the barman to make champagne cocktails (*see page 90*) and pink gins (*see page 91*).

For a 1950s table, use a pastel ▽ PVC tablecloth. Lay a runner over the cloth, place old 45s on top, and cover with clear PVC.

50s & 60s Coffee Bar Party

EVOKE THE ERA OF SWINGING COFFEE BARS, WHEN THE BEACH BOYS SURFED THE SUMMER AWAY.

Costumes Bomber jackets, white T-shirts and jeans, hooped petticoats, pedal-pushers and twin sets.

Decor Deck the room in pastel blues and pinks. Hire a juke box and clear space for jiving.

Music Elvis, Frankie Avalon and The Beach Boys.

Food Burgers, fries and ice-cream sundaes.

Drinks Cappuccinos, milkshakes and ice-cream sodas.

INFORMAL PARTY MENU

CHEESE TWISTS (*SEE PAGE 88*)
BRUSCHETTA WITH TOPPINGS (*SEE PAGE 89*)

•

ASPARAGUS & LIME PASTA (*SEE PAGE 94*)

•

CHARGRILLED CHICKEN WITH FIGS (*SEE PAGE 99*)
MINTED POTATO SALAD (*SEE PAGE 104*)
PESTO COUSCOUS SALAD (*SEE PAGE 105*)

•

CHOCOLATE TART (*SEE PAGE 108*)

PANCAKE PARTY

SERVE A RANGE OF SWEET AND SAVOURY FILLINGS FOR GUESTS TO EAT WITH PANCAKES.

Invite Write the invitation on a parcel label, then attach to a fresh lemon with a length of raffia.

Food Offer a selection of delicious fillings. These could include grated cheeses, creamed mushrooms and asparagus, ice cream and nuts, maple syrup, chocolate, lemon and sugar.

Entertainment Ask guests to help you in flipping the pancakes in the frying pan. See who can toss the pancake highest and still catch it in the pan.

COSTUME IDEAS FOR A 1970s NOSTALGIA PARTY

*Platform shoes ★ Crocheted outfits ★ Mini- and maxi-skirts
Hot pants ★ Dungarees ★ Kaftans ★ Glitter and gold lamé
Blue eyeshadow ★ Capes and long scarves ★ Denim jackets
Bell-bottom jeans ★ Culottes ★ Long hair
Beards ★ Cheesecloth ★ Wooden beads ★ Sandals
Safety pins ★ Torn clothes ★ Leather jackets*

GREAT COMPANY IS THE ESSENCE OF AN ENJOYABLE EVENT, AND A PARTY WITH CLOSE FRIENDS CAN BE AS FORMAL OR INFORMAL AS YOU CHOOSE. WHETHER PLANNING A VALENTINE'S DAY SURPRISE, A LUNCH, BRUNCH OR DINNER PARTY, ENSURE GUESTS FEEL SPECIAL BY MAKING THE ROOM AND FOOD LOOK SPECTACULAR.

INTIMATE PARTIES

GIVE A DINNER CELEBRATION AN INTIMATE RESTAURANT-FEEL BY SERVING FOOD ON OVER-SIZED WHITE PLATES, OR SET DISHES ON CO-ORDINATED CHARGER PLATES. OIL LAMPS OR CANDLELIGHT CREATE INSTANT ATMOSPHERE; MAXIMIZE LIGHTING BY SURROUNDING AN AREA WITH PLENTY OF MIRRORS, OR ALTERNATIVELY ARRANGE TINY FAIRY LIGHTS AROUND A ROOM OR GARDEN.

VALENTINE'S DAY

FOR BREAKFAST, FILL THE ROOM WITH
FRESH BLOOMS, THEN COOK SMOKED
SALMON AND SCRAMBLED EGGS, AND
SERVE ON HEART-SHAPED TOAST.

VALENTINE'S SUPPER

SURPRISE YOUR VALENTINE BY TRANSFORMING A
ROOM AT HOME INTO A BISTRO FOR THE NIGHT.

Invite Request your Valentine's presence by sending
a menu in a Valentine's card.

Decor Lay the table with a white cloth and scatter with
red rose petals. Light the room with scented candles.

Food Serve a gourmet meal for two, preparing as much
as possible in advance. Begin with herby garlic mixed
olives (*see page 89*), crudités and champagne. Follow
with oysters, seared tuna (*see page 100*) and, for dessert,
passion fruit sorbet.

20 APHRODISIACS

THE FOLLOWING FOODSTUFFS ARE REPUTED
TO HAVE APHRODISIAC PROPERTIES:

*Asparagus ★ Caviar ★ Oysters
Pomegranates ★ Lobster ★ Camel milk
Bird's nest soup ★ Cockles ★ Eels
Ginseng ★ Saffron ★ Truffles ★ Mussels
Chocolate ★ Anchovies ★ Scallops ★ Steaks
Figs ★ Clams ★ Bull's blood*

ROMANTIC SURPRISES

SHOW HOW MUCH YOU CARE BY TREATING YOUR
PARTNER TO A VALENTINE'S DAY TO REMEMBER.

*Pick up your partner in a chauffeur-driven limousine
Hire a cottage in the countryside ★ Take your partner to Paris,
Venice, New York, Fiji or Honolulu ★ Send a red rose on the hour
Declare your love in a newspaper advert
Book a box at the theatre ★ Enjoy lunch on a river boat
Treat your partner to a massage or Turkish bath*

△ VALENTINE'S DAY TREATS

★ FOR A MESSY SURPRISE, fill a Valentine's card with tiny
heart-shaped confetti, cut from red tissue paper (*see above*).
Send the confetti with a card made by sewing around two
red felt heart shapes. Stuff, scent with lavender oil, stick on to
a plain, hand-made card, and fill with the confetti.

★ SERVE A VALENTINE'S MEAL from hand-decorated
plates. Paint white china with hearts, cupids, arrows and
roses, using thermohardening water-based ceramic paint.

★ A VALENTINE'S PIZZA indulges those who prefer the
simpler things in life. Cut a large heart shape out of pizza
dough, and top with your partner's favourite fillings.

PARTIES FOR FRIENDS

SOME OF THE BEST PARTIES BEGIN AS A QUIET NIGHT WITH FRIENDS, SO WHEN THROWING AN INFORMAL, INTIMATE PARTY, TRY NOT TO OVER-PLAN.

THE PUDDING CLUB

DESSERTS, CHOCOLATE AND SWEETS CAN BE THE BEST PART OF A MEAL, SO INVITE FRIENDS TO A DINNER CONSISTING ONLY OF THEIR FAVOURITE PUDDINGS.

Invite Attach invitations to miniature boxes of truffles or chocolates.

Food Serve tiny portions of each dessert, so that guests can try a few. Offer hazelnut meringue gâteau (*see page 108*), tiramisu (*see page 109*), peach melba trifle (*see page 111*), tarte au citron (*see page 112*), and any other favourite desserts.

Drinks Serve dessert wines with the puddings. After the meal, offer coffee flavoured with cardamom or cinnamon.

NAPKIN ROSES

△

WHEN BEST FRIENDS PARTY TOGETHER, it's good to put thought into small details – even the napkins. To make a napkin rose, spread out a red or pink two-ply paper napkin, and make a 10cm (4in) fold down the left-hand side. Loosely roll the napkin up from the bottom edge around the index finger of your left hand. Wrap the layers loosely enough for there to be a small gap between each. Tightly pinch the napkin at the end of your index finger, and remove your finger. Hold the napkin beneath the flower and form a stem by twisting each hand in opposite directions. Repeat with several napkins and place the napkin roses in a vase or basket.

LADIES' PAMPERING EVENING

ASK FRIENDS TO CONTRIBUTE A SET SUM OF MONEY, AND HIRE A BEAUTICIAN, HAIRDRESSER AND MASSEUR TO COME TO YOUR HOME FOR THE EVENING.

Spend the evening with a small group of close friends, catching up on news while enjoying treatments and swapping beauty tips. Buy ready-made snacks, or make canapés in advance and refrigerate or freeze them for later.

Throw a party at which everyone dresses as and impersonates one of their closest friends for the evening.

BACKWARDS BASH

INVITE FRIENDS TO JOIN YOU FOR A DINNER PARTY IN REVERSE.

Invite Send out invitations written back-to-front (*see page 30*).

Food Serve the entire meal backwards, starting with coffee and mints, and ending with olives and canapés.

Drinks Meet guests at the door with a glass of port, and finish the evening with aperitifs.

QUIZ NIGHT

PIT YOUR GUESTS' WITS against each other by holding a quiz night at home. Ask questions on categories such as general knowledge, history, sport and films. Hold a music round, where you play a few seconds from well-known records or CDs, and ask guests to guess the artist, song title and year of release. Award prizes to the winners.

ARMCHAIR SPORTS

ARRANGE AN AFTERNOON WITH FRIENDS, WATCHING A TELEVIZED SPORTS MATCH.

Invite friends to join you on the day of a televized football match, motor racing event or baseball match. Serve chips, pizza and beer, and encourage friends to dress in their team's colours and to bring whistles and horns to cheer the teams on.

GAMES EVENING

ASK EVERYONE to arrive with a couple of favourite board games. Separate guests into different teams and hold a tournament to see which team is the outright winner. For a noisier evening, intersperse board games with more active ones, such as two-man bluff (*see page 19*) and pass the bottle (*see page 47*).

Hold a hat party, where guests must wear their silliest hat all evening.

ICEBREAKERS

★ SEAT EVERYONE around the dinner table before serving the meal, and ask each person in turn to tell a secret about themselves – the funnier the secret, the better.

★ ASK THE FIRST PERSON at a party to open the door to the next guest. They can chat together until the second guest has to answer the door to the third guest. Continue until everyone has arrived.

PERSONALIZED CHAIRS

SURPRISE CLOSE FRIENDS who often come round for supper by personalizing chairs with their names. To do this, make spare covers out of canvas to fit over chair backs. Stencil friends' names on the canvas (*see Personalized Napkins, page 78*) and put the chair backs in place before your guests arrive.

HOUSE-WARMING

INVITE FRIENDS TO EARN THEIR SUPPER BY HELPING YOU TO PAINT YOUR HOME.

When you move into a new home, persuade friends to help with the decorating. Ask guests to bring paint brushes and rollers, and then all work for an hour or two, stripping wallpaper and painting. Reward everyone by cooking an enormous meal after all the hard work.

DINNER PARTY MENU

SMOKED SALMON TRIANGLES
(SEE PAGE 95)
•
MONKFISH & BACON KEBABS
(SEE PAGE 101)

TUSCAN BEAN SALAD (SEE PAGE 104)

ROAST SWEET POTATOES
(SEE PAGE 107)
•
CHOCOLATE ROULADE
(SEE PAGE 109)

GREEK DANCING PARTY

ENJOY A FUN, NOISY EVENING EATING DELICIOUS *MEZE* AND DRINKING RUSTIC WINE.

Offer simple *meze*-style food, such as tzatziki, stuffed vine-leaves, feta salad and herby garlic mixed olives (*see page 89*). Drink wine, retsina or ouzo, then link arms in a circle and dance to Greek folk music.

◁ *Make origami table decorations using coloured paper, and use them as place settings.*

OYSTERS & GUINNESS

CELEBRATE THE DAY OF IRELAND'S PATRON SAINT, ST. PATRICK, ON MARCH 17TH.

Drink glasses of Guinness, eat oysters, and serve a traditional Irish stew. Light the room with oyster candles (*see page 31*), and dance the night away to the sound of the fiddle and pipes.

MORE ICEBREAKERS

★ AS GUESTS ARRIVE, pin the name of someone famous to their backs. Each guest must discover who they are by asking questions to which others can only answer "yes" or "no".

★ INVITE EACH GUEST at a supper party to chat to the stranger on their right. After a set time, ask everyone to introduce their partner in turn, revealing three newly discovered interesting facts about them.

WINE-TASTING PARTY

ASK FRIENDS TO BRING BOTTLES OF WINE OF DIFFERENT VALUES AND COUNTRIES OF ORIGIN.

Buy a selection of bread, crackers, cheese and fruit to eat, and provide paper, pens and glasses. Cover the wine labels and taste the wines, inviting guests to award marks out of ten. End the evening by revealing the country and cost of the wine, and who bought which bottle.

A TEA PARTY IS A CHARMING SETTING FOR A GATHERING OF FRIENDS; USE IT TO CELEBRATE SUMMER SPORTS DAYS, AUTUMNAL AFTERNOONS OR COSY WINTER DAYS IN FRONT OF A FIRE. THERE IS A HUGE VARIETY OF TEAS TO CHOOSE FROM: SELECT A BLACK OR GREEN TEA FROM INDIA, AFRICA OR CHINA, AND SERVE IT

TEA PARTIES

WITH MILK OR FRESH LEMON SLICES, OR CHILL AND SERVE IN TALL GLASSES OVER CRUSHED ICE. IDEAL ACCOMPANIMENTS FOR TEA ARE INDIVIDUAL CAKES, PASTRIES AND SANDWICHES. THE PERFECT CUCUMBER SANDWICH IS MADE WITH CAREFULLY BUTTERED, WAFER-THIN SLICED BREAD, FILLED WITH DELICATE SLICES OF CUCUMBER, AND CUT INTO DAINTY TRIANGLES.

SUMMER TEA DANCE

TRANSFORM A ROOM INTO A PALM COURT TO RECREATE THE HEYDAY OF THE TEA DANCE CIRCA 1910. HIRE A STRING QUARTET AND SPEND THE AFTERNOON DANCING THE WALTZ AND FOXTROT.

Invite Use gold calligraphy on embossed white card. Enclose a dance card for each female guest.

Decor Fill the room with pot plants. Clear an area for dancing and hang a glitter ball above the dance floor.

Table Cover a large table with a crisp white linen cloth, and use silverware and china to display sumptuous sweet dainties.

Food Salmon pinwheels (*see page 86*), cheese twists (*see page 88*), mini meringues (*see below and page 115*) and Madeira cake (*see page 117*), all served from a tea trolley.

Drinks Age a cheap plastic urn with a verdigris or pewter paint kit and use it as a bowl for a fruity summer punch or Long Island Iced Tea.

For iced tea, pour 1l (1¾pt) of cold lemonade over 3tbsp Ceylon tea leaves. Cover, stir and chill overnight. Strain, add sugar to taste and slices of lemon. Serve over crushed ice.

SPORTS MATCH HIGH TEA

ENJOY A SUMMER AFTERNOON OF SOFTBALL, ROUNDERS OR CRICKET. BRING ALONG PLENTY OF SUPPORTERS AND ENJOY A HIGH–TEA PICNIC SITTING AROUND THE PITCH.

Invite Send attached to score cards.

Decor Picnic on linen tablecloths or padded beach mats (*see page 80*). Make the meal as elegant or relaxed as you wish. For a formal afternoon, use linen napkins and pastry forks, while, for an informal tea, pack large bowls of popcorn and finger food treats, and beakers for cold drinks.

Food Quiches (*see page 86*), mini picnic pies (*see page 97*), salads, bread, cheeses, fruit loaves and a selection of home-baked cakes (*see menu, right*).

Games Play frizbee after the meal.

TEA PARTY DECOR ▷

★ Cheer up a plain white tea service by decorating it with thermohardening water–based ceramic paint. Try freehand painting (*see right*), or make a simple stamp to print with by carving a design into an eraser or potato (*see page 79*).

★ Old cups, saucers and other matching pottery make lovely vessels for candles to sit in. Drip a little wax into the base of a tea cup and stand a short, fat candle in the base. Or place each candle in a small foil dish first, so that the teacup remains free of wax.

★ Easy to construct, a simple, tiered cake stand is ideal for displaying larger cakes and smaller, individual dainties. Make the stand by selecting three attractive china plates of differing sizes. Place two upturned glass bowls between the plates, stacking them with the smallest plate on top. Alternatively, replace each bowl with four plaster pillars set in a square.

HIGH TEA MENU

CUCUMBER SANDWICHES

SAVOURY SCONES (*SEE PAGE 88*)

•

HONEY SANDWICHES

ICED FANCIES (*SEE PAGE 115*)

MINI MERINGUES (*SEE PAGE 115*)

TRIPLE CHOC COOKIES (*SEE PAGE 116*)

LUXURY FRUIT CAKE (*SEE PAGE 116*)

•

DARJEELING, CEYLON AND CHINA TEAS

ICED TEA (*SEE OPPOSITE*)

MAD HATTER'S TEA PARTY

THRILL GUESTS WITH AN AFTERNOON PARTY AT WHICH EVERYTHING IS LARGER OR SMALLER THAN LIFE. SET UP SMALL TABLES AND CHAIRS FOR CHILDREN, AND DECORATE THE AREA WITH GIANT PAINTED TEA CUPS.

Invite Cut card into the shape of a top hat and write the details along the brim.

Costumes Guests should arrive wearing hats, and be dressed in clothes that are either too large or too small.

Decor Stamp napkins and tablecloths with heart shapes (*see page 79*) and tie helium balloons around the venue.

Food Offer summer berry tarts (*see page 112*), gingerbread (*see page 114*) and iced fancies (*see page 115*).

Games Play musical cushions (*see page 47*), and pass the hat: guests pass a hat from head to head, to music, and whoever is left wearing the hat when the music stops is out. The game continues until there is a winner.

ICE BOWL ▷

A DELICATE ICE BOWL MAKES THE PERFECT CENTREPIECE FOR A SUMMER TEA TABLE, AND IS DECEPTIVELY SIMPLE TO MAKE.

1 Stand a large glass bowl in a sink and tape a smaller plastic bowl inside, so that the top of both bowls will be level when water is poured between them.

2 Pour bottled or filtered water to fill the gap between the bowls. Either leave the water clear, or arrange flower petals or fruit slices between the bowls. Place a couple of weights or tin cans inside the small bowl, and freeze.

3 When the water has frozen, fill a sink with hot water and immerse the bowls up to their rims for 10 seconds. Remove, and twist the larger bowl away from the ice.

4 Fill the small bowl with hot water, leave for 10 seconds, and carefully lift it away from the ice bowl. Freeze the ice bowl until it is needed.

To make a tea toddy to drink in colder weather, mix one part Cointreau with five parts hot tea. Pour into glasses and garnish with orange slices studded with cloves.

FLOWER CENTREPIECE

TRY MIXING FLOWERS with fruit and vegetables to make a contemporary, colourful table decoration. Stand a small square glass tank inside a larger square glass tank, then push whole red chillies, slices of orange, lemon or lime, or even small pebbles and seashells in the gap between the vases. Finally, fill the inner vase with water and add a posy of tulips or narcissi.

COLOURED GLASS VASES

KEEP EMPTY MINERAL WATER BOTTLES: blue or green coloured glass bottles in interesting shapes make ideal vases for single stems or branches of willow. To make a table centrepiece, stand several differently sized bottles in a group, fill with water and arrange with branches of willow or blossom, tulips, irises and long grasses.

EASTER

EVERYONE LOVES RECEIVING FLOWERS AT EASTER, AND A POSY IS EASY TO MAKE. TAKE A BUNCH OF NARCISSI, TULIPS, OR OTHER LONG-STEMMED FLOWERS, HOLD THEM TIGHTLY IN ONE HAND AND ARRANGE LARGE ORNAMENTAL OR SAVOY CABBAGE LEAVES BENEATH THE FLOWER-HEADS. SURROUND THE POSY WITH TISSUE PAPER AND TIE WITH RIBBON.

EASTER TEA

CELEBRATE EASTER BY THROWING A TEA PARTY IN YOUR HOME FOR FRIENDS AND FAMILY.

Invite Write on lengths of wide yellow ribbon, then tie them around small posies (*see below*).

Decor Fill the room with vases of fresh flowers, and hang blown eggs from tree branches.

Food Offer hot-cross buns, and bake tarte au citron (*see page 112*), blueberry muffins (*see page 114*) and a luxury fruit cake (*see page 116*).

Entertainment Spend the afternoon painting and staining blown eggs (*see below*). Hide tiny foil-wrapped chocolate eggs around the garden and send the children on an Easter egg hunt.

◁ ## STAINED EASTER EGGS

BLOWING EGGS IS A TRADITIONAL EASTER PASTIME WHICH CHILDREN LOVE. THIS IS A BEAUTIFULLY DELICATE VARIATION ON PAINTING BLOWN EGGS.

1 Hold an egg over a bowl and prick a hole in either end with a needle. Use a cocktail stick to enlarge the holes, then push it inside the egg to pierce the yolk. Blow into the rounded end of the egg, catching the contents in the bowl. Rinse the egg with cold water and leave to dry.

2 Wet a selection of tiny flowers and lay them, good-side down, on the egg shell, smoothing the petals flat. Carefully cover the flowers with onion skins before slipping the egg inside an old stocking and tying it tightly to keep the onion skins in place.

3 Put the wrapped egg in a pan of cold water, bring to the boil and boil for 10 minutes. Remove from the water and leave the egg to cool before cutting away the stocking. Peel away the onion skins and discard the flowers to reveal the flower-printed egg.

KEEP CHILDREN'S PARTIES SHORT AND FUN; CHILDREN ARE EASILY TIRED, SO LIMIT A PARTY TO A COUPLE OF HOURS BUT PACK IT FULL OF EXCITING ACTIVITIES, WHETHER BOWLING, SWIMMING OR ICE SKATING. DECIDE WELL IN ADVANCE ON THE THEME, VENUE, NUMBERS, FOOD AND PARTY BAGS, AND

CHILDREN'S PARTIES

ORGANIZE GAMES, WITH PRIZES FOR EVERY CHILD. ALLOW CHILDREN TO DRAW UP THE GUEST LIST AND TO DECIDE WHAT FOOD TO SERVE ON THE DAY. ENSURE THAT THE AFTERNOON IS FILLED BY DRAWING UP A PARTY TIMETABLE. ENLIST AS MUCH HELP AS POSSIBLE FROM FRIENDS, AND CONSIDER HIRING A CHILDREN'S ENTERTAINER, SUCH AS A MAGICIAN, PUPPETEER OR CLOWN.

FANCY DRESS IDEAS

Cowboys ★ Astronauts and space invaders
Clowns ★ Pirates ★ Animals
Cops and robbers ★ Monsters ★ Home-made hats
Nursery rhymes ★ Teddy bears' picnic
Hallowe'en ★ Fairytales ★ Footballers
Caribbean island ★ 1970s disco
National dress ★ Kings and queens
Explorers ★ The future

20 PLACES FOR A CHILDREN'S PARTY

Circus ★ Zoo ★ Fairground
Swimming pool ★ Children's farm ★ Sporting event
Theme park ★ Cinema ★ Bowling alley
Ice rink ★ Castle ★ Safari park
Dry ski slope ★ Water park ★ Go-kart course
Seaside ★ Double-decker bus ★ Picnic site
Puppet show ★ Restaurant

CHILDREN'S NAPKIN IDEAS

MAKE A CHILDREN'S PARTY TABLE A RIOT OF COLOUR
BY USING PAPER NAPKINS TO THEIR FULL POTENTIAL.

★ Make biscuit beds as place settings. Lay a folded napkin
on a table and lift one of the loose corners towards you,
pressing it down in place. Write a child's name on a parcel
label, tie it around the neck of a gingerbread man and slip
him under the napkin flap so he looks as if he is in bed.

★ Swag parcels make pretty wrappings for small table gifts.
Lay a coloured paper napkin, good side down, on a table
and place a small present in the centre. Draw up the corners
of the napkin and secure the gift with a tied ribbon.

★ To make candy-cane napkins, lay two co-ordinating
napkins on top of each other, one corner pointing towards
you. Slide the top napkin 2.5cm (1in) away from you, so you
can see two edges of the napkin beneath. Starting at the
nearest corner, roll the napkins away from you. When you
reach the top corner, fold in half and stand in a beaker.

MEXICAN PIÑATA ▷

HANG A PIÑATA DONKEY FROM A TREE AND ALLOW
EACH CHILD IN TURN TO TRY, BLINDFOLDED, TO HIT
IT WITH A STICK, RELEASING THE TREATS INSIDE.

1 Blow up a large balloon. Fold a sheet of newspaper
into a strip 10cm (4in) wide and tape it around the centre
of the balloon. Using wallpaper paste, stick five layers of
torn newspaper on to the balloon, avoiding the knot.

2 When the newspaper is dry and hard, glue on legs made
from cardboard rolls, and a head and neck shaped from
cones of card. Cut a small hole in the top of the body, pop
the balloon and remove. Fill the belly with sweets and gifts.

3 Cut about 30 long strips of coloured crêpe paper 10cm
(4in) wide. Lay two strips on top of each other, fold in half
lengthways, and machine-sew down the centre. Fold along
the stitched line and cut a fringe, taking care not to cut the
stitching. Cover the donkey in glue and wind crêpe paper
strips around to cover it completely. Add ears, eyes and a
saddle. Thread wire through the piñata and hang up.

◁ ## PARTY-BAG GIFTS

DON'T FORGET TO PACK PARTY BAGS FOR CHILDREN
TO TAKE HOME. FILL THE BAGS WITH FAVOURITE
SWEETS, TOYS, GAMES AND MAGIC TRICKS.

Slice of birthday cake ★ *Balloons*
Yo-yo ★ *Water pistol* ★ *Coloured chalks*
Mini toy animal ★ *Packet of cards*
Sugar mice ★ *Face-painting crayons*
Dot-to-dot book ★ *Chocolate coins* ★ *Dice*
Pot of bubbles ★ *Toy handcuffs* ★ *Joke book*
Whoopie cushion ★ *Poster paints and brushes*
Colouring book ★ *Novelty-shaped eraser*
Plastic vampire teeth ★ *Magic tricks* ★ *Lollypops*
Marbles ★ *Sugared almonds*

BISCUIT-BAKING PARTY

AS CHILDREN LOVE TO BAKE, HOLD A PARTY WHERE
THEY MAKE, BAKE AND DECORATE THEIR OWN BISCUITS.

Invite Attach invitations to gingerbread men (*see page 114*)
wrapped in cellophane.

Costumes Sew chef's hats and aprons for everyone to wear
when they are baking. Allow children to take these home at
the end of the afternoon.

Entertainment Buy a selection of farmyard-shaped biscuit
cutters, shaped as ducks, cats, cows, pigs and gingerbread
people. Let everyone join in making and rolling out the
dough and stamping out the shapes. When the biscuits have
been baked, give each child their own farmyard of biscuits to
decorate with small sweets, sugar strands and tubes of
coloured icing. Award prizes for the best-decorated biscuits,
and let children take their creations home in party bags.
Give the biscuit cutters as gifts in the bags.

PARTY FOOD

KEEP FOOD SIMPLE: CHILDREN LIKE TO GRAZE AND
EAT WITH THEIR FINGERS. GIVE MORSELS APPEAL BY
OFFERING MINI-VERSIONS FOR SMALL MOUTHS.

★ To make children's ice lollies, fill small plastic or paper
beakers with orange juice or squash, and freeze until
slushy. Stand a lolly stick in the centre of each beaker
and freeze. When solid, carefully squeeze out the lollies.

★ To make sailing boat jellies, scoop out the fruit from
orange halves. Fill the halves with jelly and fruit. When set,
quarter the oranges and add a cocktail-stick mast and a sail.

GAMES

FILL A CHILDREN'S PARTY WITH PLENTY OF GAMES, AND BE SURE THAT EVERY CHILD WINS A PRIZE BY THE END OF THE DAY.

CHINESE WHISPERS

SIT CHILDREN in a circle and whisper a message into one child's ear. The child whispers it into the ear of the next child, and so the message is passed round the circle. The last child to receive the message says it out loud, and it is compared to the message the first child was given.

SQUEAK PIGGY, SQUEAK

A CHILD stands in the centre of a seated circle of children, and is blindfolded and spun around. The child must then find a seated child and identify them by sitting on their lap and asking them to "squeak piggy, squeak". The chosen child should squeak, disguising their voice. A child correctly named goes into the centre; if not, the first child starts again.

BEACH GAMES

ENJOY A DAY at the beach, playing beach Olympics. Mark out a start and finish line, then divide children into teams and play three-legged, piggy-back, wheelbarrow and sack races. Ask children to bring hats and swimming costumes, and don't forget buckets, spades, water pistols, sun block and a first-aid kit.

Award children medals made of chocolate discs wrapped in foil and tied with ribbon.

WHO AM I?

MAKE PAPER HATS and write the name of a famous person or fictional character on each. Sit children in a circle and place a hat on each head, without letting them see the name on it. Children take it in turns to ask each other questions that require a yes or no answer. Each child continues questioning until they guess something incorrectly. The next child in the circle then starts asking questions.

LEMON RELAY

DIVIDE CHILDREN into two teams and mark a start and finish line. The first child in each team has to roll a lemon up the room and back, using only a pencil. When they finish, they pass the pencil and lemon to the next child, who continues the race. The lemon and pencil should be passed in relay down the whole team. The first team to roll the lemon home wins the race.

FIRE! FIRE!

LINE UP two teams. Put a full bucket of water in front of each line and an empty bucket at the back. When a whistle is blown, the first child in each line scoops up water from the bucket into a beaker and passes it to the back of the line, where the water is poured into the bucket. The empty beaker is then passed back to the front. The first team to empty the bucket of water is the winner. This game is best played outdoors!

DOODLING GAMES

COVER A DINING TABLE with brown paper. Trace around plates, cutlery and glasses using wax crayons, and add children's names as place settings. Stand the crayons in plastic cups, and place around the table for children to doodle with over lunch.

BABY PARTIES

DECORATE BABIES' FIRST PARTY INVITATIONS WITH PRINTS OF THEIR HANDS AND FEET.

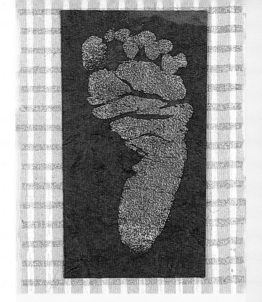

Let babies scribble their own Christening invitations. Colour-photocopy and mount on thick card.

◁ BABY FOOTPRINT

IMMORTALIZE A NEW BABY BY TAKING A FOOTPRINT.

Paint the baby's foot with embossing ink. Print by pressing the foot on to a sheet of paper, making sure the toes are as flat as possible. Sprinkle embossing powder on the wet print, tap off the excess, and heat with an electric paint stripper or hair dryer, so it melts and looks embossed. Repeat with your baby's hands if you wish.

SENSORY PARTY

CRAWLING BABIES AND TODDLERS LEARN BY TOUCH AND FEEL, SO THROW A PARTY THEY'LL LOVE.

Create a sensory room by arranging cardboard boxes, cardboard tubes, pages from old magazines, tissue paper and foil trays on the floor. Thread scrunched foil balls and bells on to string and hang from a door frame. Blow bubbles and hand out wooden spoons and saucepans for children to have fun making a racket with.

NAMING CEREMONY PRESENT IDEAS

Adopt a baby animal
Silver box for milk teeth
Name a star ★ Silver bookmark
Cross-stitched sampler of the baby's name and birthday
Minted coin set ★ Bank account
Stencilled child's stool (*see page 81*)
Silver bangle

WATERBABY PARTY

OLDER BABIES ARE FASCINATED BY EACH OTHER, SO MEET WITH OTHER PARENTS, AND LET YOUR CHILDREN GET TO KNOW EACH OTHER.

Appoint a meeting time at a local swimming pool. Bring inflatables and rubber ducks, and encourage babies to splash and swim around under your close supervision. Invite the other parents back to your house afterwards for tea and cakes.

BABY SHOWER PARTY

CELEBRATE AN IMPENDING BIRTH BY ORGANIZING A BABY SHOWER.

Invite Send with a photo of the very pregnant mother-to-be.

Food Ask everyone to bring a different dinner course.

Entertainment Bring gifts for the new baby or pampering treats for the expectant mother. Friends could club together to buy a car seat or crib.

TREE-PLANTING PARTY

MARK THE BIRTH OF A BABY BY PLANTING A TREE IN HIS OR HER HONOUR.

When the baby is one month old, invite grandparents and friends to join you in planting a sapling. Take a picture of everyone with the new baby in front of the tree.

INDIVIDUAL DECORATIVE TOUCHES, SUCH AS STYLED NAPKINS, TABLECLOTHS AND TABLE PLACE SETTINGS, MAKE A PARTY SPACE LOOK REALLY SPECIAL. PAY AS MUCH ATTENTION TO DECORATING TABLE LEGS OR REVAMPING GARDEN FURNITURE AS YOU DO TO PARTY FOOD, AND YOU WILL CREATE AN OCCASION TO REMEMBER.

FINISHING TOUCHES

USE COLOURS AND DECOR TO REFLECT A PARTY THEME, WITH BRIGHT OCHRES AT A FIREWORKS PARTY, OR DELICATE FLORAL FABRICS AT A SUMMER BABY SHOWER. DON'T NEGLECT LIGHTING IN A ROOM: CREATE THE RIGHT AMBIENCE WITH CANDLES AND SPOTLIGHTS. CUSTOMIZE FABRIC, PLATES AND GLASSES WITH YOUR OWN HAND-CRAFTED DESIGNS TO COMPLETE THE SETTING.

INVITATIONS

CREATE AND SEND OUT HAND- CRAFTED INVITATIONS TO GIVE YOUR PARTY A UNIQUE, PERSONAL TOUCH THAT GUESTS WILL LOVE.

BUTTON INVITATIONS

Print invitations on small rectangles of white card. Cut white tulle fabric or tracing paper to the same size as each card. Attach the fabric to the top of the front of the card with a mother-of-pearl button and white thread.

CO-ORDINATED INVITATIONS

Decorate stationery with a hand-made stencil. Choose an idea from the party theme, taking inspiration from a swatch of fabric or a fruit or flower, and draw the design on to clear acetate. Cut out the design using a scalpel, and transfer on to good-quality writing paper using a stencil brush and acrylic paint. Cut the printed paper to size for use as invitations, menus and place cards.

PICTURE PERFECT INVITES

Use a passport photo booth to take pictures of the party hosts. Take as many photos as there are guests. If you are sending out wedding invitations, take photos of the bride and groom wearing a tiara and top hat. Print the text on co-ordinating paper and mount on card below the photo.

PLATE INVITATIONS

For an outdoor party, write directly on to paper plates using coloured marker pens. Post the plates to guests.

RIBBON INVITATIONS

Fold a rectangle of white card in half and punch two holes in the folded side. Thread with coloured ribbon and tie in a bow.

PAPER CRAFTS

GO TO TOWN DECORATING PAPER, WHETHER FOR USE AS WRAPPING OR TO COMPLEMENT DINNER-TABLE DECOR.

LEAF PRINTS

Press leaves overnight between the pages of a book. To decorate glasses, thinly brush the veined side of a leaf with emulsion paint and print on to a rectangle of white card. When the prints are dry, cut out the leaf shape, leaving a rectangle of card at the bottom of the leaf. Make two cuts in the bottom of the card, and use these to slot the print on to a wine glass or tumbler. To make leaf wrapping paper, print leaves on tissue paper.

DECORATED NAME BADGES

For a large-scale party where few guests know each other, mail out attractive name badges with the invitations, stamping the badges with rubber stamps (*see Customized Paper, right*).

PAPER PHOTOGRAPH ALBUM

Customize the front of a photograph album using photosensitive paper. Gather a selection of shells, pressed flowers and leaves, and lay them on the light-sensitive paper. Leave the paper exposed to direct sunlight or a strong lamp for five minutes, then remove the objects and wash the paper to remove the light-sensitive coating. Glue or stitch three rows of three clear PVC pouches to the front of a photo album. Cut out the paper to fit the pouches and slip an image into each pouch.

CUSTOMIZED PAPER

Cut an image out of an eraser and use to stamp cards, paper and gift tags, using coloured or embossing ink.

CHERUB INVITATIONS ▷

1 Mix together 3 cups sifted plain flour, 1 cup salt, 1 cup water to form a soft and pliable, but not sticky, dough. Knead the dough for five minutes until smooth and roll out.

2 Shape the dough into cherubs 10cm (4in) long (*see right*). Arrange the cherubs on oiled baking sheets and bake for 8 hours, or overnight, at 110°C/225°F/Gas ¼.

3 Let the dough cool on the baking sheets, then paint and varnish the cherubs and stick to invitation cards.

◁ MUSICAL GIFT-WRAP

1 Buy a gold cardboard gift box, or paint a plain box a metallic colour and allow to dry.

2 Cut out strips of music from an old musical score and glue the strips randomly to the box.

3 When the glue is dry, complete the gift-wrap by placing a present inside the box and securing it by tying with a long length of shimmering ribbon.

PAPER MOSAIC TABLE ▷

1 Cut a sheet of MDF or plywood to the same size as a table top. Paint with emulsion paint and allow to dry.

2 Cut coloured card or sticky paper into 2cm (¾in) squares. Draw a simple design on the MDF or plywood, and paste the coloured squares on to the design, trimming to fit where necessary.

3 Give the finished mosaic a coat of clear varnish to seal and protect it, then place on the table.

NAPKINS

USE FLOWERS OR FOLD NAPKINS TO MATCH A PARTY THEME AND, FOR AN EXTRA-SPECIAL FINISH, STENCIL ON GUESTS' INITIALS.

WATERLILY NAPKINS

Fold each corner of an open napkin in to meet the centre, then repeat twice. Turn the napkin over and fold the four corners into the centre. Hold the centre flat and bend one corner towards the centre, until a point from the layer beneath is free. Tug the freed point upwards, until it softly wraps around. Repeat to create four petals, then pull the points up from beneath these to make eight petals.

FLORAL NAPKINS

Iron fabric napkins, fold them in half, then roll into sausage shapes. Tie each napkin with wide ribbon and tuck a flower head beneath the ribbon. Use flowers that do not wilt, such as gerberas, carnations and chrysanthemums.

DAISY-CHAIN NAPKINS

Draw a six-petal daisy with a stem and two leaves on a plain linen napkin. Stitch around the design using yellow and green silk in chain-stitch, then iron the napkin.

PERSONALIZED NAPKINS

Draw a guest's initials in italic script on to white paper. Lay a sheet of clear acetate on the paper, and trace the initials with indelible pen. Cut out the traced initials using a craft knife, then lightly spray the back of the acetate stencil with spray mount and stick it to a fabric napkin. Paint through the stencil using fabric paint, applying it with a small sponge or brush. Remove the stencil. When the fabric paint is dry, use a hot iron to fix it.

PLATES & GLASSES

GIVE GLASSES ADDED GLAMOUR BY EMBELLISHING THEM WITH FROSTED PATTERNS, GOLD RELIEF PAINT OR GLASS GEMS.

CHARGER PLATES

For a stylish occasion, serve dinner plates on top of co-ordinated charger plates, or spray cheap larger plates with silver or gold paint to create opulent chargers.

FLOWER CHARGERS

Sit a dinner plate on a large charger plate, and tuck flowers, herbs and leaves between the edges of the two plates.

ICE TRAY

Fill a plain, shallow metal tray with mineral water or filtered water. Set slices of lemon, lime and parsley in the water and place the tray in the freezer until the water is frozen solid. Arrange *fruits de mer* on the ice and serve.

BANANA-LEAF PLATTERS

To serve canapés or a Moorish or Roman banquet, dispense with plates and serve food on trays of banana or vine leaves.

RIBBON-THREADED PAPER PLATES

Using a hole punch, make 16 evenly spaced holes around the edge of each plate. Thread with ribbon and tie in a bow.

BREAD BOWLS

Serve soup from hollowed-out round bread loaves. Cut the top off individual loaves and scoop out the bread to leave a 1cm (½in) crust. Brush the entire loaf and lid, inside and out, with egg white and bake at 160°C/325°F/gas 3 until crisp. You can eat the bowls after eating the soup.

Sweetheart Napkins ▷

1 Use a small, sharp knife to score a heart shape on the cut edge of one half of a potato.

2 Cut away the potato surrounding the heart shape, to leave a raised image. Blot the shape on kitchen paper to rid it of moisture.

3 Print on a napkin by dipping the potato in fabric paint. Add a checked border by dipping a square of potato in another colour. When the design is dry, iron to fix. Roll up and tie with a wooden heart threaded on raffia.

◁ Etched Glasses

1 Wrap a clean glass with strips of fine masking tape to create the outline of the desired pattern. To make a spotted glass, cut circles of masking tape 2cm (¾in) wide.

2 Spray the glass with etching spray, available from craft shops. The spray will turn the unmasked areas of the glass opaque.

3 Leave the glass to dry, then peel away the masking tape to reveal the design. Rinse the glass before use.

Jewelled Goblets ▷

1 To make a luxurious, gem-encrusted goblet, first spray a plain beaker with gold paint.

2 When the paint is dry, use gold relief paint to cover the beaker with a swirled pattern.

3 Glue fake glass or plastic gems to the beaker to resemble precious stones. Use the goblets with a matching tablecloth (*see Opulent Tablecloth, page 81*).

FABRIC IDEAS

SWATHE A DINNER TABLE IN FABRIC

TO GIVE THE PERFECT BACKDROP

DESIGNED FOR THE OCCASION

FOR A PARTY BANQUET OR FEAST.

WEIGHTED TABLECLOTH

To ensure a tablecoth does not blow away during an outdoor party, sew attractive objects to the hem to weigh it down. Attach items such as seashells, glass beads and small weights, sewn on with coloured silk or cord.

TABLE RUNNER

Rectangular tables look great dressed with a table runner. Cover a table with an ironed white cloth. Cut a long strip of fabric at least 50cm (19½in) wide and 1m (40in) longer than the table. Hem the fabric, iron, and lay down the centre of the table. Co-ordinate napkins and flowers with the runner, or arrange individual flowers in coloured mineral water bottles down the length of the runner.

RAFFIA BEACH MAT

Cheap raffia beach mats make excellent tablecloths for outdoor parties, and can be laid on the floor at picnics. Paint pebbles with bright emulsion paint and use to hold the mat in place.

PEBBLE-PRINT BEACH MAT

Iron a large square of canvas or heavy-duty cream fabric. Halve a selection of different-sized potatoes and blot them with kitchen paper. Prepare grey, pale blue, pale red, brown and orange fabric paints in separate shallow bowls. Dip the potatoes in the paints and print pebble shapes on the fabric, overlapping the prints, so that little fabric is visible. When dry, iron to fix. Back the mat with wadding and a layer of water-resistant fabric or an old ground sheet, then sew the three layers together.

TABLES & CHAIRS

BRING FURNITURE TO LIFE BY PAINTING

IT WITH SWAGS OF SCENTED

IT IN BOLD COLOURS, OR DECKING

FLOWERS OR EVERGREENS.

FLORAL TABLE SWAG

Cut chicken wire 75cm (29in) wide and slightly longer than the table. Lay blocks of 10cm (4in) thick florist's foam along one long edge of the wire. Roll the wire around the foam to make a sausage shape. Bend the wire in the centre to give a swag shape. Arrange cut flowers in the holes in the wire, pushing the stems into the foam. Use larger blooms in the centre of the swag. Tie the ends with ribbon and hang along a table.

BEAUTIFUL TABLE LEGS

Dress up a table by wrapping wide strips of co-ordinating ribbon, crêpe paper or long lengths of trailing ivy up the legs. Secure with bows of coloured ribbon.

WINTER LIGHTED TABLE

Make a table swag (see left) from evergreens, holly and ivy, and loop it along the length of a table. Lightly spray the swag with fake snow, then weave tiny white fairy lights along its length, securing them with ribbon bows. Sprinkle the swag with orange or pine oil, so the heat from the lights scents the room.

PAINTED GARDEN FURNITURE

Brighten plastic garden furniture with flower, spot or leaf patterns. Wash furniture in hot, soapy water then spray with heavy-duty aerosol paint. Cut a pattern into a sponge to form a stamp (see Daisy-stamped Tablecloth, right), dip into a contrasting acrylic paint colour, and stamp on the design.

Opulent Tablecloth ▷

1 Select a length of silk, crushed velvet or brocade in purple, deep blue, red or dark green.

2 Add intricate designs using gold or silver metallic paint in a swirled pattern, leaving the centre empty and including small shapes to decorate with fake gems. Dry flat, then stick glass or plastic gems to the small shapes.

3 Embellish the tablecloth further by trimming it with gold or silver bobble or bullion braiding. Use the tablecloth with matching beakers (*see Jewelled Goblets, page 79*).

◁ Daisy-stamped Tablecloth

1 Cut the shape of a daisy petal from a sponge-backed scouring pad or a potato, using scissors or a sharp knife.

2 Dampen the sponge in water and squeeze dry. If using a potato, blot on kitchen paper. Tip white fabric paint in a dish, dip the stamp in lightly, and stamp on a plain cloth. Re-coat every 2–3 prints.

3 Stamp the centre of the daisies with a cotton bud dipped in yellow fabric paint. Iron the dry design.

Child's Milking Stool ▷

1 Little milking stools make memorable gifts for children at a party. Buy one unvarnished wooden stool per child and paint brightly with emulsion paint.

2 Make a stencil (*see Personalized Napkins, page 78*) and stencil a design or name on each stool.

3 Seal the stools with three coats of clear varnish. Use the stools for musical chairs at a children's party, then present them to children when they leave.

FLOWERS & FRUIT

TO COMPLETE A DINNER PARTY AND TABLE LINEN WITH SETTING, ADORN THE ROOM FLOWERS AND FRUIT.

GILDED TREES

Hang bay trees with gilded pears, lemons or limes to create a delightful room decoration. If using citrus fruit, wash first in hot soapy water to remove any wax, then dry well. Spray the fruit with gold aerosol paint and attach to the bay tree by threading with 25cm (10in) lengths of flexible wire, twisting the wire around tree branches and cutting off excess wire. Lightly spray the bay tree with gold paint and leave to dry.

FLOATING FRUIT BOWL

Fill a shallow, attractive glass bowl with assorted, halved fruit, such as lemons, clementines and kumquats, halved side down. Top up the bowl with water and dot with floating candles in co-ordinating colours. Scatter the water with gerbera petals.

FRUIT-STAMPED LINEN

Stamp linen with fruit for a harvest party or wedding; use white paint on calico or beige fabric for a stunning effect. Iron the cloth and lay flat. Cut apples and pears in half lengthways, blot the cut side on kitchen paper, and coat with fabric paint. Press the fruit firmly and evenly on to the fabric, then carefully repeat to form a pattern. When dry, fix the design with a hot iron.

LAVENDER CANDLE COLLARS

Tie together 10 stems of lavender, just under the flowers, with wire, and trim the stems short. Repeat to make seven bundles. Bend wire loosely around a candle and remove the candle. Wire the lavender to the wire circle. Put a candle in a candle holder and place the lavender over the candle, to rest on the holder.

LIGHTING

STORE CANDLES FOR A LARGE PARTY CANDLES LAST LONGER, AND THEY IN A FRIDGE OR COLD ROOM – COOLER WILL GLOW INTO THE NIGHT.

LACY CANDLES

Embellish plain white candles with a pattern of gold or silver spray paint. Cut a length of lacy paper doily to fit around a candle. Fix in place with masking tape and spray with gold or silver aerosol paint. Leave the paint to dry before removing the paper doily.

SUMMER LANTERNS

Light up a garden party in summer by painting plain glass jars. Decorate the jars with translucent glass paint in a variety of bright colours, then allow to dry. Loop a long piece of string to make a handle, then wrap the rest of the string around the jar rim and tie the ends in a knot. Hang the jar from a tree.

VEGETABLE CANDLES

To make unusual outdoor table decorations, tie baby vegetables, such as carrots or courgettes, around fat church candles. Keep the vegetables in place as you work, with an elastic band wrapped around the candle. When complete, tie raffia around the vegetables and remove the elastic band.

ORANGE CANDLES

Cut a thin slice from the top of an orange, stand a night-light on the cut end and score around its shape using a serrated knife. Remove the night-light and scoop the flesh out from inside the scored circle, using the knife and a teaspoon. Stud the orange with cloves and set the night-light inside.

FLOWER DECOUPAGE ▷

1 Press delicate flowers such as pansies and daisies in blotting paper between the pages of a heavy book. Leave to dry out for a few weeks.

2 Thin some PVA glue with water, and paint very lightly on to a terracotta pot painted white. Position the flowers on the outside of the pot, pressing them gently in place.

3 When dry, give the flowers a light coat of thinned PVA glue or varnish to protect them.

◁ DRIED APPLE WREATH

1 Cut apples into 3mm (⅛in) thick slices. Soak the slices for 10 minutes in a bowl with 1 small cup of lemon juice, 1½tbsp salt and enough water to cover.

2 Dry the slices on kitchen paper and bake on wire racks at 140°C/275°F/Gas 1 for 5–6 hours, checking them regularly. Remove when the slices are leathery but not browned. Leave to cool.

3 Thread the slices with rag bows on 45cm (18in) wire. Join the ends to form a wreath.

FLOATING CANDLE CENTREPIECE ▷

1 Wine glasses make ideal containers for floating candles. Stand some inexpensive wine glasses, or a selection of different-sized glasses, on a circular mirror.

2 Dye some water with food colouring, then fill each wine glass with the water.

3 Float a small candle, in a co-ordinating colour to the water, on top of each glass. Complete the centrepiece by arranging glass beads on the mirror.

THERE ARE OVER 100 DELICIOUS RECIPES IN THIS SECTION WHICH CAN BE USED FOR ANY OCCASION, FROM PICNICS AND TEA PARTIES TO BANQUETS & BALLS. AS WELL AS TRADITIONAL AND SEASONAL PARTY FAVOURITES, THERE ARE SOME TWISTS ON CLASSIC DISHES AND A NUMBER OF NEW RECIPES, TO ENABLE

FOOD & DRINK

YOU TO CHOOSE FOOD & DRINK FRIENDS AND FAMILY WILL LOVE. ENTERTAINING SHOULD BE FUN, SO THE RECIPES AND DRINKS FEATURED ARE ALL QUICK TO PREPARE YET GIVE IMPRESSIVE RESULTS. THIS WILL ENSURE THAT YOU WON'T BE STUCK IN THE KITCHEN AT YOUR OWN PARTY, BUT CAN CIRCULATE FREELY AND HAVE AS GOOD A TIME AS YOUR GUESTS.

CANAPÉS & DRINKS

CANAPÉS AND FINGER FOODS ARE IDEAL FOR SERVING AT COCKTAIL PARTIES, INFORMAL DRINKS AND PICNICS. MANY CAN BE PREPARED IN ADVANCE, GIVING YOU TIME TO CHECK THAT EVERYONE'S DRINKS ARE TOPPED UP, AND TO JOIN IN THE FUN.

SALMON PINWHEELS

A MODERN VERSION OF A CLASSIC. THESE SALMON ROLLS (TROUT WORKS JUST AS WELL) CAN BE MADE AND CHILLED UP TO 24 HOURS IN ADVANCE. SLICE JUST BEFORE SERVING.

MAKES 30

200g (7oz) full-fat cream cheese • grated zest of 1 lemon freshly ground black pepper • 2tbsp snipped chives 225g (7½oz) sliced smoked salmon or smoked trout

1 Beat together the cream cheese, lemon zest, black pepper and chives until smooth.

2 Lay the strips of salmon or trout on a work surface. Spread the cheese mixture on to the salmon and roll up, as if making mini Swiss rolls. Slice thinly into pinwheels.

MUSHROOM BUNDLES

THESE ARE VERY QUICK AND SIMPLE TO MAKE. THEY CAN BE ASSEMBLED IN ADVANCE AND CHILLED OVERNIGHT, OR FROZEN FOR UP TO A WEEK. COOK JUST BEFORE SERVING.

MAKES 24

150g (5oz) button mushrooms • 90g (3oz) cream cheese with herbs 100g (3½oz) filo pastry • 2tbsp olive oil

1 Preheat the oven to 200°C/400°F/Gas 6. Remove the stalks from the mushrooms. Place a spoonful of cream cheese in the centre of each mushroom.

2 Cut each sheet of filo in half, brush with oil and place a mushroom in the centre. Draw the pastry corners over the mushroom to make a bundle, pinching to seal. Bake for about 5 minutes, or until golden.

CARAMELIZED ONION QUICHES

MAKES 20

250g (8oz) shortcrust pastry • 3 onions • 3tbsp olive oil 1tsp caster sugar • 2 medium eggs • 150ml (¼pt) single cream salt and freshly ground black pepper • 2tbsp freshly chopped thyme

1 Preheat the oven to 200°C/400°F/Gas 6. Roll out the pastry on a lightly floured surface. Using a 7.5cm (3in) fluted cutter, cut out 20 rounds and use to line patty tins. Chill in the fridge for 10 minutes. Line the pastry cases with scrunched foil and bake blind for 5 minutes.

2 Finely chop the onions and fry with the oil and sugar for about 15 minutes in a covered pan, over a gentle heat, until golden. Stir frequently to prevent sticking. Spoon the onion mixture into the pastry cases.

3 Beat together the eggs, cream and seasoning. Divide between the onion quiches and sprinkle with thyme. Bake for 15–20 minutes or until puffy and set.

VARIATIONS

SUNDRIED TOMATO: Use only 1 onion, together with 4 chopped sundried tomatoes, and continue as directed.

ASPARAGUS & FRESH PEA: Blanch 200g (7oz) asparagus, trimmed and halved, with 175g (6oz) peas. Arrange in the pastry cases. Combine 3 tablespoons snipped chives, 3 medium eggs, 300ml (½pt) double cream, and season. Pour over the asparagus and peas and bake for 25–30 minutes.

LARGE QUICHE: Line a 20cm (8in) round quiche tin with the pastry. Line with scrunched foil and bake blind for 15 minutes. Remove the foil and return to the oven for a further 10 minutes. Fill and bake for 25–30 minutes.

SALMON PINWHEELS

MUSHROOM BUNDLES

SAVOURY
SCONES,
TOPPED WITH
SALAMI,
PROSCIUTTO
AND SMOKED
SALMON

CARAMELIZED
ONION QUICHES

SALMON PINWHEELS

SAVOURY SCONES

TO MAKE SWEET SCONES, OMIT THE CHEESE AND ADD
30G (1OZ) EACH OF SUGAR AND MIXED DRIED FRUIT.
TOP WITH JAM, CREAM AND BERRIES.

MAKES 18

300g (10oz) self-raising flour • 100g (3½oz) butter, diced
100g (3½oz) fontina cheese • 1 medium egg • 150ml (¼pt) milk
FOR THE TOPPINGS
200ml (7fl oz) crème fraîche • 6 slices smoked salmon
6 slices salami • 6 slices prosciutto
fresh herbs, such as dill, marjoram and thyme, to garnish

1 Preheat the oven to 220°C/425°F/Gas 7. Sift the flour into
a bowl and rub in the butter. Finely grate the cheese and
add it to the bowl with the egg and milk. Mix to a soft, but
not sticky, dough. Roll on a floured surface to 2.5cm (1in)
thick, and cut out 18 rounds. Put on a greased baking sheet
and bake for 12–15 minutes or until golden. Leave to cool.

2 Halve the scones and add a little crème fraîche and
half a slice of topping to each. Garnish with herbs.

CORNBREAD

SERVE THIS SLICED, TOASTED AND CUT INTO TRIANGLES,
DRIZZLED WITH CHILLI SAUCE OR EXTRA-VIRGIN OLIVE OIL.

MAKES ONE 500G (1LB) LOAF

1 medium egg • ½tsp saffron strands • 350ml (12fl oz) buttermilk
90g (3oz) butter, melted and cooled • 175g (6oz) plain flour
125g (4oz) fine cornmeal (polenta) • 1tbsp baking powder
2tsp caster sugar • 1tsp fine salt • 3tbsp poppy seeds

1 Preheat the oven to 200°C/400°F/Gas 6. Butter a 500g
(1lb) loaf tin, and line the base with greaseproof paper.

2 Beat together the egg, saffron, buttermilk and melted
butter. Sift the flour, cornmeal, baking powder, sugar
and salt into a bowl. Make a well in the centre and stir
in the egg mixture and the poppy seeds.

3 Spoon the mixture into the prepared tin and bake for
about 30 minutes, or until risen and cooked through.

4 Leave to cool in the tin for 5 minutes before
transferring to a wire rack to cool completely.

PUFF PASTRY PIZZAS

YOU CAN FREEZE THE PASTRY DISCS IN ADVANCE,
THEN TOP AND BAKE THEM ON THE DAY.

MAKES 20 SMALL PIZZAS

400g (13oz) puff pastry • 8 medium tomatoes, sliced
3 cloves garlic, sliced • 2tsp sea salt
60ml (2fl oz) olive oil • fresh basil leaves, to garnish
60g (2oz) Parmesan • 20 pitted black olives, halved

1 Preheat the oven to 220°C/425°F/Gas 7. Roll out the
pastry thinly on a floured surface. Using a 7.5cm (3in)
fluted cutter, cut 20 circles from the pastry and place on
a baking sheet. Arrange the tomatoes and garlic on top.
Sprinkle with the sea salt and olive oil, and bake for
10–12 minutes or until golden.

2 Garnish with basil leaves. Use a vegetable peeler to
shave pieces of Parmesan on to the pizzas. Scatter
with the black olives and serve warm.

CHEESE TWISTS

ANOTHER GREAT PARTY STANDBY. USE PESTO, RED PEPPER
OR SUNDRIED TOMATO PASTE AS AN ALTERNATIVE TO
CHEESE. CHILDREN LOVE THESE MADE WITH MARMITE.

MAKES 40

400g (13oz) puff pastry • 1 medium egg, beaten
100g (3½oz) mature Cheddar or Parmesan, finely grated
2tbsp sesame seeds • 2tbsp poppy seeds

1 Preheat the oven to 220°C/425°F/Gas 7. On a lightly
floured work surface, roll out the pastry thinly into
a large rectangle. Brush with the beaten egg to within
1cm (½in) of the edge. Sprinkle with the cheese.

2 Fold the pastry in half and roll gently with a rolling
pin. Sprinkle half the pastry with sesame seeds and the
other half with poppy seeds. Cut the pastry into thin fingers
using a sharp knife and twist each finger at both ends.

3 Arrange on a baking sheet and bake for about
12-15 minutes or until golden. You can make and
chill these up to 24 hours in advance, or freeze them
for up to a month before baking.

HERBY GARLIC MIXED OLIVES

225g (7½oz) black olives • 225g (7½oz) pimento-stuffed green olives
3 cloves garlic, sliced • 250ml (8fl oz) extra-virgin olive oil
half a lime, sliced • a few sprigs thyme
freshly ground black pepper

Mix all the olives in a bowl, then add all the other ingredients, seasoning with black pepper. Mix well, cover with clingfilm and chill for at least 48 hours.

BRUSCHETTA

SERVES 6

1 olive ciabatta loaf, sliced • 3tbsp extra-virgin olive oil
2 cloves garlic, crushed • freshly ground black pepper

FOR THE TOPPINGS

300g (10oz) mushrooms in oil • 3tbsp snipped chives
3tbsp black olive tapenade • 200g (7oz) canned cannellini beans
300g (10oz) mixed peppers and sundried tomatoes in olive oil
2tbsp chopped fresh oregano • 6 slices salami
12 black olives • 4tbsp mascarpone cheese
100g (3½oz) mozzarella, sliced • grated zest of 1 lemon
fresh marjoram, to garnish • 2tbsp olive oil

1 Brush one side of each bread slice with olive oil, sprinkle with garlic, season with black pepper, then grill until golden. Turn the slices over, prepare the other side in the same way and grill until crisp and golden.

2 To serve, either put a selection of toppings in small bowls and let guests help themselves, or make a platter of ready-topped bruschetta as follows:

★ Drain the mushrooms and arrange on the bruschetta. Season with black pepper and garnish with snipped chives.

★ Spread the tapenade over the bruschetta and top with drained cannellini beans.

★ Drain the peppers and sundried tomatoes and arrange on the bruschetta. Season and sprinkle with the oregano.

★ Curl each slice of salami and arrange on the bruschetta, garnished with black olives, mascarpone and oregano.

★ Arrange the mozzarella on the bruschetta, sprinkle with lemon rind and marjoram, and drizzle with olive oil.

BLINI WITH QUAIL'S EGGS & SMOKED FISH

THESE SMALL RUSSIAN PANCAKES ARE TRADITIONALLY MADE USING BUCKWHEAT FLOUR. THIS RECIPE IS A DELICIOUS, LIGHTER VERSION MADE WITH STRONG PLAIN FLOUR.

SERVES 6

FOR THE BLINI

175g (6oz) strong plain flour • 1tsp salt • 1 sachet easy-blend
dried yeast • 1 medium egg, separated • 200ml (7fl oz) tepid water
200ml (7fl oz) milk • 30ml (2tbsp) sunflower oil

TO COMPLETE

12 quail's eggs • 225g (7½oz) smoked salmon
200ml (7fl oz) crème fraîche • 100g (3½oz) lumpfish roe
a few sprigs fresh chervil • 1 lemon, cut into wedges
ground cayenne pepper

1 Sift the flour into a bowl, add the salt, then stir in the dried yeast. Beat the egg yolk with the water and stir into the flour. Whisk the egg white until it is stiff but not dry, and fold into the flour mixture. Cover the bowl and leave to stand for 30 minutes.

2 Heat the milk until it just begins to steam, then beat it into the flour mixture to form a batter. Cover the bowl again and leave the batter for a further 30 minutes or until it is well risen and bubbly.

3 Meanwhile, to cook the quail's eggs, place them in a pan of lightly salted water, bring to the boil and simmer for about 4 minutes, then shell and cut in half.

4 To cook the blini, heat a frying pan and wipe it with kitchen paper dipped in a little of the oil. Drop in spoonfuls of the batter to make pancakes measuring about 7.5cm (3in) in diameter.

5 Cook for 1–2 minutes on each side, until golden and cooked through. Keep warm while cooking the remaining blini, wiping the pan with a little more oil as necessary.

6 Serve the warm pancakes topped with the quail's eggs, smoked salmon, crème fraîche, lumpfish roe, fresh chervil and lemon wedges, and a sprinkling of cayenne pepper.

DRINKS WITH A KICK

◁ **BUCKS FIZZ:** Squeeze the juice of 6 large oranges into a jug. Pour a little of the fresh orange juice into each glass and top up with champagne. To take this drink to picnics, squeeze the orange juice into a rigid plastic container, and surround a bottle of champagne or sparkling white wine with plenty of ice packs. Serves 10.

◁ **PIMM'S:** To prepare the flavourings, wash and halve 300g (10oz) strawberries; thinly pare the zest from 2 lemons; thinly slice 5cm (2in) cucumber (having discarded the seeds); segment 2 clementines (skin and pith removed). Stir these into a jug containing 300ml (½pt) Pimm's. Cover and leave for up to 1 hour before topping up with 900ml (1½ pints) chilled sparkling white wine or lemonade, and borage ice cubes (*see below*). Serves 10.

BORAGE ICE CUBES: Quarter fill an ice-cube tray with cold water, set a borage flower in each cube and freeze for 1 hour. Top up with iced water and freeze until solid.

CHAMPAGNE COCKTAILS: Pour 30ml (2tbsp) of either crème de cassis, brandy or sloe gin into each glass and top up with champagne.

BANANA DAIQUIRI: Blend together 60ml (4tbsp) white rum, 30ml (2tbsp) crème de banane, 30ml (2tbsp) orange juice, 15ml (1tbsp) lime juice, a quarter of a fresh, mashed banana, 5ml (1tsp) whipping cream and 1tsp caster sugar. When thoroughly blended, add a glass of crushed ice and briefly blend again. Garnish with banana slices and serve with a wide straw. Serves 1.

MARGARITA: Decorating the glass is a key part of serving margaritas. Dip the rim of a long-stemmed, wide-brimmed cocktail glass in a dish of lime juice and then into fine salt. Attach a thin half slice of lime to the rim. Then, in a cocktail shaker packed with ice, shake together 60ml (4tbsp) tequila, 45ml (3tbsp) triple sec and 15ml (1tbsp) lemon or lime juice. Strain, leaving the ice behind, and serve. Serves 1.

SEA BREEZE: Combine 45ml (3tbsp) vodka, 60ml (4tbsp) grapefruit juice and 90ml (6tbsp) cranberry juice. Shake in a cocktail shaker with a glassful of crushed ice. Pour into a glass and garnish with slices of lime. Serves 1.

APPLE WHIZZ: Mix together equal quantities of well-chilled  apple juice and dry cider. Serve each glass decorated with slices of apple.

MULLED WINE: The secret of making good mulled wine is not to overheat it. It is ready to serve just as the steam rises and before the liquid bubbles. Traditional mulled wine is made by heating a bottle of red wine in a saucepan, together with a sliced orange, a stick of cinnamon and 3–4 cloves. Some people add sugar or sliced clementines for extra sweetness, while juniper berries give a hint more fruitiness. If you want a really warming drink, add a glass of brandy to the pan just before serving. Serves 6.

PINK GIN: Coat the bottom half of a frosted glass with 4 dashes of angostura bitters and discard the excess. Add 60ml (4tbsp) gin and stir in a little iced water. Serves 1.

SANGRIA: Half fill a large jug with ice cubes. Pour in a bottle of Spanish red wine, then add 60ml (4tbsp) brandy and stir well. If desired, top up the jug with carbonated water. Decorate with sliced apricots and strawberries. Serves 6.

ALCOHOL-FREE DRINKS

CRANBERRY COCKTAIL: Squeeze the juice of 2 oranges and 1 lime. Tip the ice from an ice-cube tray into a plastic bag and crush with a rolling pin. Put the ice in a jug and pour over the fruit juice and 2tbsp clear honey. Pour into glasses and top up with cranberry juice. Decorate the glasses with wedges of orange or lime. You can make this drink in a thermos flask for picnics. Serves 6.

PASSION FRUIT MIX: Seed a honeydew melon, scoop out the flesh and place it in a food processor. Halve 3 passion fruit and sieve the juice into the processor. Blend the fruit mixture until smooth. Pour into a jug and top with chilled sparkling mineral water or lemonade. If taking this drink to a picnic, top up the fruit mixture with sparkling water or lemonade on arrival. Serves 6.

APRICOT FRUIT CUP: Mix together equal quantities of apricot juice and sparkling grape juice. Pour this mixture into jugs filled with slices of fresh apricot, strawberries cut in half, a couple of sprigs of fresh mint and plenty of ice.

STARTERS

WHETHER A SOUP THAT SUITS AN OCCASION SUCH AS HALLOWE'EN OR HOGMANAY, OR A LIGHT SUMMER TAPAS SELECTION FOR FRIENDS AND FAMILY, STARTERS SHOULD ALWAYS MAKE AN IMPRESSION, AND LEAVE YOUR GUESTS WANTING MORE.

ROASTED PEPPER & TOMATO SOUP

TRY SERVING THIS SOUP AT FIREWORKS PARTIES.

SERVES 4

2 large red peppers, halved, seeded and cut into chunks
1kg (2lb) ripe plum tomatoes, quartered • 2 cloves garlic, halved
4tbsp olive oil • sea salt, for sprinkling
300ml (½pt) vegetable stock • freshly ground black pepper

FOR THE CROUTONS
2tbsp olive oil • 1 clove garlic, halved
4 thick bread slices, crusts removed
2 sprigs rosemary, broken into pieces

1 Preheat the oven to its highest setting. Put the peppers, tomatoes, garlic and olive oil into a roasting tin and sprinkle with sea salt. Mix and then roast for about 15 minutes, stirring occasionally to ensure even cooking.

2 Transfer this mixture to a food processor and blend, gradually adding the vegetable stock, until smooth. Pour into a pan, heat gently and season to taste.

3 Meanwhile, heat the oil for the croutons in a frying pan and add the garlic. Cut the bread into cubes, add them to the pan, and stir until golden. Drain the croutons, discarding the garlic, and sprinkle with the pieces of rosemary. Divide the soup between warmed bowls and scatter the croutons and rosemary over the top.

CREAMY PUMPKIN SOUP

SERVES 6

2tbsp olive oil • 1 onion, chopped • 2tsp ground ginger
1.25kg (2½lb) pumpkin, peeled, seeded and chopped
1 large potato, peeled and chopped • 1.25 litres (2pt) vegetable stock
300ml (½pt) double cream • salt and freshly ground black pepper
2tbsp chopped fresh coriander, to garnish

1 Heat the oil in a heavy-based pan and fry the onion until softened but not coloured. Add the ginger and stir well. Add the pumpkin and potato, and stir-fry over a high heat for 5 minutes. Add the stock and bring to the boil. Simmer for 25 minutes or until the pumpkin is tender.

2 Blend in a food processor, then tip the smooth soup back into a pan and stir in the cream. Season with salt and pepper to taste and serve garnished with the chopped coriander.

COCK-A-LEEKIE SOUP

SERVES 4

2tbsp sunflower oil • 2 leeks, sliced
1tsp granulated sugar • 2 chicken breasts, cooked and shredded
125g (4oz) pitted prunes • 600ml (1pt) chicken stock
salt and freshly ground black pepper

1 Heat the oil in a pan, stir in the leeks and sugar and cook gently for 5 minutes, until the leeks have softened.

2 Stir in the chicken, prunes and stock. Bring to the boil, then reduce the heat and simmer for 10 minutes. Season with salt and freshly ground black pepper to taste.

Tapas Selection

Serves 8

Calamari

225g (7½oz) baby squid • 1 medium egg, beaten
salt and freshly ground black pepper • 1tbsp flour
300ml (½pt) sunflower oil • lime wedges

1 Cut the squid into rings, leaving the tentacles whole. Dip in a little beaten egg, then coat in seasoned flour. Heat the oil in a large, deep pan.

2 Cook the squid in batches for 1–2 minutes. Drain on absorbent kitchen paper and serve with lime wedges.

Potatoes with Chorizo & Aïoli

200ml (7floz) olive oil • 125g (4oz) chorizo, sliced
450g (1lb) small new potatoes • 1tsp coarse sea salt
2 large sprigs rosemary • 3 cloves garlic • 1 medium egg
2tbsp lemon juice • 1tsp mustard • 3tbsp sunflower oil

1 Heat 3 tablespoons of the olive oil in a pan. Stir in the chorizo and potatoes, cover and heat until the oil sizzles. Simmer gently for about 10 minutes, shaking the pan frequently. Add the salt and rosemary and cook for 5 minutes, until the potatoes are very tender.

2 To make the aïoli, blend the garlic, egg, lemon juice and mustard in a food processor, gradually adding the remaining olive oil and the sunflower oil. Season to taste. Skewer the potatoes and chorizo with cocktail sticks and serve with the aïoli.

Meatballs with Red Sauce

2 spring onions, chopped • 2 cloves garlic, crushed
450g (1lb) lean minced lamb • 30g (1oz) fresh white breadcrumbs
1 egg yolk • 2 roasted, seeded red peppers • 1 red chilli
150ml (¼pt) vegetable stock • 150ml (¼pt) double cream

1 Mix the spring onions, garlic, lamb and breadcrumbs. Mix in the egg yolk. Shape into small balls.

2 Blend the peppers, chilli, stock and cream in a processor. Bring to a simmer in a pan until hot.

3 Dry-fry the meatballs in a non-stick pan for 10 minutes, until browned. Put them in the sauce and simmer for 5 minutes. Serve with cocktail sticks.

ASPARAGUS & LIME PASTA

SERVES 4

225g (7½oz) fresh angel hair pasta • salt
250g (8oz) asparagus spears, halved • 450ml (¾pt) double cream
juice and zest of 1 lime • 2tbsp chopped fresh parsley
shavings of Parmesan, to garnish • freshly ground black pepper

1 Cook the pasta in a large pan of boiling salted water for 2 minutes, or until al dente. Blanch the asparagus in boiling salted water for 2 minutes, then drain.

2 Meanwhile, heat the cream with the lime juice and zest. Add the pasta and the asparagus to the hot cream. Spoon on to serving plates and garnish with the parsley and shavings of Parmesan. Season with freshly ground black pepper to taste.

SWEET & SOUR PRAWNS

THIS DELICIOUS RECIPE ALSO WORKS WELL WITH DICED CHICKEN OR PORK.

SERVES 6

18 whole raw king prawns • 1tbsp sunflower oil
2 shallots, finely chopped • 1 clove garlic, finely chopped
1 red chilli, seeded and finely chopped • 2tbsp tomato purée
1tbsp caster sugar • juice and zest of 1 orange • 1tbsp cornflour
salt and freshly ground black pepper • 125g (4oz) crispy seaweed

1 Carefully peel the shells from the prawns, leaving the heads and end tails intact. Remove the black vein that runs down the back of each prawn.

2 Heat the oil in a frying pan and cook the shallots, garlic and chilli for 3 minutes. Add the tomato purée, sugar and orange zest. Combine the orange juice with the cornflour, add to the pan and season. Heat until the mixture bubbles.

3 Add the prawns to the pan and cook until they have turned pink and are cooked through.

4 Cook the seaweed according to packet instructions, then serve some on each plate with the prawns on top. Spoon over the sauce.

SMOKED SALMON
TRIANGLES

SERVES 6

FOR THE TRIANGLES

90g (3oz) herb-flavoured cream cheese • 200g (7oz) cooked prawns
grated zest of 1 small lime • salt and freshly ground black pepper
12 strips of smoked salmon, each 20cm x 7.5cm (8in x 3in)

FOR THE SALAD

90ml (6tbsp) olive oil • juice of 1 small lime
2tsp Dijon mustard • small bunch basil leaves
60g (2oz) mixed salad leaves

1 Beat the cheese until smooth, then chop the prawns and fold in with the lime zest. Season to taste.

2 Lay the strips of smoked salmon on a work surface. Put a small spoonful of the cheese mixture on one corner of each strip and shape roughly into a triangle. Fold the salmon around the cheese, rolling up the strip to make neat triangles. Arrange on a tray, then cover and chill until ready to serve.

3 For the dressing, put the oil, lime juice, mustard and basil in a liquidizer or food processor and blend until the basil is very finely chopped. Season with salt and freshly ground black pepper to taste. Strain through a fine sieve into a jug.

4 To serve, sit one salmon triangle on each plate and divide the mixed salad leaves between the plates. Set a second triangle to the side and drizzle with a little dressing. Serve the remaining dressing separately.

PROSCIUTTO &
EGG MOUSSES

THESE TASTY LITTLE MOUSSES ARE QUICK TO MAKE AND CAN BE PREPARED **24** HOURS BEFORE A PARTY.

SERVES 8

250g (8oz) chive-flavoured cream cheese • 300ml (½pt) crème fraîche
12 hard-boiled eggs, chopped • salt and freshly ground black pepper
200g (7oz) prosciutto • 8tbsp snipped chives • 60g (2oz) rocket leaves

1 Beat together the cream cheese and crème fraîche. Fold in the eggs and season with salt and pepper.

2 Line 8 small ramekins with clingfilm, then with the prosciutto, leaving some overlapping the sides. Divide the egg mixture between the ramekins and cover with the overlapping prosciutto. Chill for at least 3 hours.

3 Turn out the moulds on to chilled plates. Sprinkle the chives on top and garnish with the rocket leaves.

KOFTA MEATBALLS

SERVE WITH A TOMATO SALAD, OR WITH A TOMATO SAUCE AND RICE AS A MORE SUBSTANTIAL DISH.

SERVES 6

2 cloves garlic, finely chopped • 1 onion, finely chopped
2tsp garam masala • 1tsp ground coriander
1tsp ground turmeric • 1tbsp tomato purée
400g (13oz) lean minced lamb
salt and freshly ground black pepper • 2tbsp olive oil

TO SERVE

ready-made tomato and avocado salsa • cucumber raita
6 mini pitta breads

1 In a bowl, lightly work the garlic, onion, garam masala, coriander, turmeric and tomato purée into the minced lamb. Season with a little salt and pepper.

2 With wetted hands, shape the mixture into about 24 balls. Heat the oil in a pan and cook the meatballs for about 10 minutes, turning frequently.

3 Serve hot with tomato and avocado salsa, raita, and warmed, sliced pitta breads.

MAIN COURSES

WHEN ENTERTAINING, SIMPLE DISHES, DONE WELL, ALWAYS IMPRESS. WHETHER SERVED AT A 21ST CELEBRATION OR AN IMPROMPTU GET TOGETHER, A PIZZA MADE WITH PIZZAZZ IS BETTER THAN SOMETHING MORE SOPHISTICATED THAT FALLS FLAT.

SCRAMBLED EGGS IN BRIOCHE

A MARVELLOUS LAST–MINUTE BRUNCH–PARTY DISH THAT IS ALSO WONDERFUL WHEN FRIENDS TURN UP OUT OF THE BLUE. SHOP–BOUGHT BRIOCHES ARE EXCELLENT – IT'S WORTH KEEPING PLENTY IN THE FREEZER.

SERVES 4

4 brioches
30g (1oz) butter • 4 medium eggs • 150ml (¼pt) double cream
2tbsp snipped chives • 4tbsp salmon eggs (keta caviar)
freshly ground black pepper

1 Cut the top off each brioche and scoop out the centre. Place the brioches on a baking sheet and warm through in a low oven while making the scrambled eggs.

2 Melt the butter in a heavy-based pan over a low heat. Beat together the eggs and cream. Pour the egg mixture into the pan with the melted butter and cook over a low heat until the eggs start to scramble. The secret of good scrambled eggs is to keep the heat low and to stir the eggs frequently. Don't hurry or the mixture will become rubbery.

3 Remove the scrambled eggs from the heat and mix in the snipped chives. Fill each warmed brioche with scrambled eggs and garnish with salmon eggs and freshly ground black pepper.

SIMPLE KEDGEREE

THIS DISH IS GREAT PREPARED AHEAD. IT CAN BE MADE THE NIGHT BEFORE AND POPPED INTO THE FRIDGE, READY TO HEAT UP AS GUESTS ARRIVE FOR BRUNCH. IT ALSO MAKES A TASTY SUPPER–PARTY DISH.

SERVES 4

375g (12oz) long-grain white rice • 60g (2oz) butter
1 onion, finely chopped • 450ml (¾pt) double cream
3tbsp chopped fresh dill • salt and freshly ground black pepper
6 hard-boiled eggs, chopped • 300g (10oz) smoked salmon strips
2tbsp chopped fresh coriander • 2tbsp mild curry paste

1 Cook the rice in a large pan of salted boiling water for 10 minutes or according to packet instructions.

2 Meanwhile, melt the butter in a large pan and cook the onion for about 5 minutes or until softened but not coloured. Drain the rice and stir into the onion, with 300ml (½pt) of the cream and the dill. Season with salt and black pepper, to taste.

3 Quickly fold the hard-boiled eggs and smoked salmon through the hot rice mixture and spoon it into a serving dish. Garnish with the coriander and keep warm. Heat the remaining cream, stir in the curry paste and serve with the kedgeree. (Curry sauce is the traditional accompaniment to kedgeree.)

VARIATION

LUXURY EGG & KEDGEREE FIRST COURSE: Omit the curry paste and substitute a mixture of white and wild rice for the white rice. Replace the chopped coriander with chervil and serve each portion topped with a poached egg to make an elegant starter for eight people.

PIZZA

EACH TOPPING IS ENOUGH FOR TWO PIZZAS. AS YOU GET MORE CONFIDENT, MAKE YOUR OWN TOPPINGS WITH SLICES OF SALAMI AND COMBINATIONS OF VEGETABLES. TUNA AND SWEETCORN IS A CHILDREN'S FAVOURITE.

MAKES FOUR 20CM (8IN) PIZZAS

450g (1lb) strong plain flour • 1tsp salt • 1tsp easy-blend yeast
about 300ml (½pt) lukewarm water
FOR THE TOPPINGS
2tbsp olive oil • 1 onion, chopped • 2 cloves garlic, crushed
750g (1½lb) chopped canned tomatoes
fresh basil leaves, to garnish • salt and freshly ground black pepper
THREE-CHEESE TOPPING
150g (5oz) mozzarella, sliced • 150g (5oz) goat's cheese, sliced
60g (2oz) pecorino cheese, coarsely grated
HAM & MUSHROOM TOPPING
125g (4oz) mixed mushrooms, thinly sliced
100g (3½oz) Parma ham, cut into strips
100g (3½oz) mozzarella, grated

1 To make the pizza base, first sift the flour and salt into a large bowl. Stir in the yeast and enough lukewarm water to make a soft but not sticky dough. Turn the dough out on to a lightly floured work surface and knead for 10 minutes, until smooth and elastic. Place in an oiled bowl and cover with oiled clingfilm. Leave to prove for about 1 hour in a warm place or until doubled in size.

2 Meanwhile, to make the topping, first heat the oil in a large frying pan. Cook the onion and garlic in the oil until softened but not coloured. Add the tomatoes and boil rapidly for about 15 minutes, stirring occasionally, until the tomatoes are reduced and very thick. Remove from the heat and leave to cool.

3 Knock back the dough and shape into 4 rounds, each 20cm (8in) across. Preheat the oven to 230°C/450°F/Gas 8. Spread the tomato mixture over the pizzas. Scatter the three cheeses on two of the pizzas and the mushrooms, ham and mozzarella on the other two.

4 Bake the pizzas in the preheated oven for 12–15 minutes, until the toppings are golden and the pizzas are cooked through. Garnish each pizza with fresh basil leaves and season, then serve.

MINI PICNIC PIES

MAKES 12

2tbsp sunflower oil • 1 onion, chopped • ½tsp ground cinnamon
½tsp grated nutmeg • 250g (8oz) turkey, minced
salt and freshly ground black pepper
375g (12oz) ready-rolled puff pastry • 60g (2oz) gammon,
cut into 12 cubes • beaten egg, to glaze

1 Preheat the oven to 220°C/425°F/Gas 7. Heat the oil in a pan, add the onion and cook for about 5 minutes, until softened. Add the cinnamon, nutmeg and minced turkey. Cook, stirring occasionally, until the turkey is lightly browned, about 10 minutes. Remove the pan from the heat and leave to cool. Season with salt and pepper to taste.

2 Using plain or fluted cutters, cut out 12 rounds of pastry, each 7.5cm (3in) across, and use to line patty tins. Cut 12 smaller rounds to make lids. Using a teaspoon, divide half the turkey mixture between the pastry-lined tins. Place a gammon cube in each and spoon over the remaining turkey mixture.

3 Dampen the pastry rims with a little water and press on the lids to seal. Brush the pies with a little egg and make a small slit in the top of each. Bake in the preheated oven for about 25 minutes or until puffy and golden.

VENISON & SAUSAGE HOTPOT

SERVE WITH CREAMY MASHED POTATO FOR COLD
OUTDOOR PARTIES, WHERE COMFORT FOOD IS CALLED FOR.

SERVES 6

2tbsp sunflower oil • 12 shallots, peeled and halved
2 stalks celery, sliced • 100g (3½oz) baby carrots, trimmed
450g (1lb) pork and garlic sausages • 2tsp ground allspice
1tbsp flour • 750g (1½lb) venison, cubed
juice and zest of 1 orange • 900ml (1½pt) beef or venison stock
salt and freshly ground black pepper • 2tbsp chopped fresh parsley

1 Heat the oil in a large casserole, add the shallots,
celery and carrots and fry for about 10 minutes, until
softened but not coloured. Remove the vegetables from the
casserole. Add the sausages and cook for about 5
minutes, turning frequently, until they have browned.
Remove the sausages from the casserole.

2 Mix the allspice with the flour. Toss the venison cubes
in the seasoned flour to coat. Add the venison to the
pan and cook until sealed and browned on all sides.

3 Return the vegetables and sausages to the pan with
the orange juice and zest and the stock. Mix well,
then cover with a lid and cook until the venison is tender,
about 45 minutes. Season to taste, then stir in the chopped
parsley and serve with creamy mashed potatoes.

VARIATION

BEEF IN BEER: Replace the venison and sausages with
1kg (2lb) lean cubed beef and substitute beer for the
stock, following the instructions above.

QUICK CASSOULET

SERVES 8

8 duck breasts, halved • 8 chicken drumsticks
2 onions, chopped • 3 cloves garlic, crushed
225g (7½oz) rindless streaky bacon, chopped
750g (1½lb) canned cannellini beans, drained
750g (1½lb) chopped canned tomatoes • 300 ml (½pt) chicken stock
3tbsp chopped fresh marjoram and oregano
175g (6oz) salami, thickly sliced
salt and freshly ground black pepper • fresh oregano, to garnish

1 Place the duck breasts in a large casserole and heat
on the hob. Cook on each side until browned, about
8 minutes. Remove the duck from the casserole and pour
off all but 1 tablespoon of the duck fat. Add the chicken
drumsticks to the pan and cook for 10 minutes or until
golden on all sides. Remove from the casserole.

2 Add the onions, garlic and bacon to the casserole,
and stir for 5 minutes or until the onion has softened.
Return the duck and chicken to the casserole and stir in
the beans, tomatoes, chicken stock, chopped herbs and
salami. Bring to the boil then simmer for about 1 hour
or until the meat is tender.

3 Season with salt and freshly ground black pepper,
and garnish with oregano. Serve with mashed root
vegetables or potatoes, or crusty bread and a salad.

SMOKED CHICKEN

SERVES 4

2tbsp lapsang souchong tea leaves • 1 litre (1¾pt) boiling water
1 medium-sized chicken • 1 lemon, sliced • 2 star anise
1 cinnamon stick, broken

1 Put the tea leaves into the boiling water and mix well.
Place a wire rack over a large frying pan or wok. Lay
the chicken on the rack and pour over the tea. Scatter the
chicken with the lemon slices, star anise and cinnamon
stick, then bring the tea back to the boil.

2 Cover the pan with greaseproof paper and simmer
for about 1 hour or until the chicken is cooked
through. Serve with rice and stir-fried vegetables.

CHARGRILLED CHICKEN WITH FIGS

THIS DISH IS BEST SERVED WITH GREEN SALAD LEAVES,
A MINTED POTATO SALAD, AND PESTO ON THE SIDE.

SERVES 6

6 chicken breasts, part-boned • 6tbsp redcurrant jelly
2tbsp light soy sauce • 2tbsp coarsely chopped rosemary
2 cloves garlic, finely chopped • salt and freshly ground black pepper
3tbsp olive oil • 9 baby aubergines, sliced lengthways
9 fresh figs, halved

1 Make slits through the skin and flesh of the chicken and place in a shallow dish. Beat together the redcurrant jelly, soy sauce, rosemary, garlic, seasoning and 1 tablespoon olive oil. Pour the mixture over the chicken, cover and chill for at least half an hour, preferably overnight, turning the chicken once.

2 Heat half the remaining oil in a griddle pan and cook the chicken until well browned on each side, then set aside. Heat the remaining oil in the griddle and cook the aubergine slices on both sides until lightly browned.

3 Return the chicken to the griddle and continue cooking until tender. Quickly heat the fig halves in the pan and serve with pesto and salad.

CHICKEN TIKKA

COOKING INDIAN FOOD IS VERY EASY WITH SO
MANY EXCELLENT READY-MIXED CURRY PASTES
AVAILABLE IN SUPERMARKETS.

SERVES 6

6 chicken breasts, boned and skinned
300g (10oz) chicken tikka paste • 150ml (¼pt) natural yogurt
1tbsp olive oil • 1 onion, chopped • 2 cloves garlic, chopped
TO SERVE
2.5cm (1in) piece cucumber, finely diced • juice of ½ lime
2tbsp chopped fresh mint • naan bread

1 Cut the chicken breasts into bite-sized pieces. Mix together the paste and half of the yogurt and use to coat the chicken. Cover and chill for at least 30 minutes or overnight if possible.

2 Heat the oil in a pan and fry the onion and garlic until softened and lightly coloured. Add the marinated chicken and fry for about 15 minutes, until the chicken is tender and cooked through.

3 Mix the remaining yogurt with the cucumber, lime juice and chopped mint. Serve with the chicken, accompanied with Chickpea Dhal (*see page 106*), rice and the warmed naan bread.

POACHED SALMON IN ASPIC.

THE PERFECT DISH FOR SUMMER BUFFET CELEBRATIONS, THIS IS ONE OF THE FEW CLASSIC RECIPES THAT IS MUCH EASIER TO MAKE THAN IT LOOKS.

SERVES 8

1 fresh salmon weighing about 2.5kg (5lb)
1 bottle white wine • 1 shallot, sliced
1 lemon, cut into 4 segments • 1 bay leaf • 2 sticks celery,
cut into large chunks • 8 white peppercorns • 2tbsp parsley stalks
FOR THE LIME MAYONNAISE
150ml (¼pt) mayonnaise • grated zest and juice of 1 lime
4tbsp chopped fresh mixed herbs, such as parsley,
tarragon, chervil and dill
TO COMPLETE
22g (¾oz) packet of aspic • 1 cucumber, halved and thinly sliced
flat-leaf parsley, to garnish

1 Cut the fish in half just in front of the large fin on the top of its back. Put both halves in a large roasting tin. Add the white wine and enough water just to cover the salmon. Scatter the fish with the shallot slices, lemon segments, bay leaf, celery, peppercorns and parsley stalks. Cover the fish tightly with a large sheet of foil.

2 Put the roasting tin on the hob and slowly bring the liquid to the boil, about 10 minutes. Simmer for 5 minutes, then remove from the heat. The salmon will continue to cook as it cools in the liquid.

3 Carefully remove the salmon from the tin. Strain and reserve the liquid. Peel away the skin from the sides of the fish. Carefully remove the fillets from the bone and set aside. (Don't worry if the fillets fall apart, the fish will be stuck together with the mayonnaise.)

4 Beat together all the ingredients for the mayonnaise. Use it to stick the boned fish back together again, then chill. Use the reserved liquid to make up the aspic according to packet instructions. Chill until it just starts to set.

5 Brush the salmon with a layer of aspic. Arrange the cucumber slices down the sides of the fish to look like scales. Brush with more layers of aspic, then chill for up to 6 hours. Garnish with flat-leaf parsley just before serving.

VARIATION

COULIBIAC: Another summer celebration salmon dish that is very easy to serve and popular at smart buffets.

★ Cook a 500g (1lb) salmon fillet as described above. Divide 500g (1lb) puff pastry in half. Roll one portion 2.5cm (1in) larger than the salmon fillet and the other 5cm (2in) larger than the fillet. Set the salmon on the smaller piece of pastry.

★ Sprinkle the salmon with 75g (2½oz) cooked long grain rice, 75g (2½oz) finely chopped spinach and 4 sliced hard-boiled eggs.

★ Brush the rim of the pastry with a little beaten egg yolk and set the remaining piece on top, pressing the edges together to seal. Use any pastry trimmings to make scales.

★ Bake in a preheated oven at 220°C/425°F/Gas 7 for 30 minutes. Serve with the lime mayonnaise.

SEARED TUNA

QUICK AND EASY TO PREPARE, THIS DISH IS A TASTY OPTION FOR AN IMPROMPTU GATHERING.

2 medium-sized tuna steaks • 2 sprigs rosemary
1tbsp olive oil • salt and freshly ground black pepper

1 Preheat a griddle pan or frying pan. Rinse the tuna steaks, pat dry, then make tiny slits in the flesh. Break off small pieces of rosemary and gently press them into the slits. Brush the steaks on both sides with the oil and season with salt and black pepper.

2 Cook the tuna steaks for about 3 minutes on each side, or according to taste – the tuna should be sealed on the outside but still pink on the inside. Serve with steamed vegetables.

LAMB BURGERS

THESE ARE VERY EASY TO MAKE. REPLACE THE LAMB
WITH MINCED QUORN FOR A VEGETARIAN ALTERNATIVE.

SERVES 8

1kg (2lb) minced lamb • 1tbsp mint jelly • 1 clove garlic, crushed
1 shallot, finely chopped • salt and freshly ground black pepper
FOR THE SAUCE
1 large red onion, chopped • 2tbsp olive oil
375g (12oz) chestnut mushrooms, chopped
300ml (½pt) double cream • 1tbsp flour
TO SERVE
8tbsp tomato relish • 8 sesame seed baps • green salad leaves

1 Mix together the minced lamb, mint jelly, garlic and
shallot, then season with salt and pepper. Divide the
mixture into 8 and pat into rounds. Cook under a hot
grill or over a barbecue for 5 minutes on each side.

2 To make the sauce, fry the onion in the oil until
softened, then add the mushrooms and simmer until
all the liquid from the mushrooms has evaporated. Blend
the cream with the flour, add to the pan and mix well.
Simmer the sauce for 5 minutes or until thickened.

3 Put 1 tablespoon of tomato relish in each bap and
add a layer of salad leaves. Top with the hot burger,
spoon the mushroom sauce on top, then add the lid.

MONKFISH &
BACON KEBABS

MONKFISH HAS WONDERFULLY FIRM FLESH, MAKING IT
IDEAL FOR THREADING ON KEBAB SKEWERS. WRAP THE
FISH IN BACON TO KEEP IT MOIST AND FULL OF
FLAVOUR. YOU WILL NEED 12 SKEWERS.

SERVES 6

250g (8oz) rindless streaky bacon • 3tbsp sundried tomato paste
750g (1½lb) monkfish tail fillets, cubed • 6 large shallots, quartered
12 black olives • 2tbsp olive oil • a few sprigs thyme
salt and freshly ground black pepper

1 If using wooden skewers, soak them in water for
15 minutes. Preheat the grill to its highest setting. Lay
the bacon rashers on a board and spread thinly with the
tomato paste. Wrap each monkfish cube in a bacon rasher
and thread on to the skewers, alternating with the pieces
of shallot. Thread a black olive on the end of each skewer.

2 Mix the oil and thyme together and season with
salt and freshly ground black pepper. Brush over the
kebabs and grill for 2–3 minutes on each side, brushing
with more of the flavoured oil as necessary.

TREACLE GLAZED HAM

SERVE WITH COURGETTES WITH GARLIC (PAGE 107) OR
POMMES DAUPHINOIS (PAGE 106).

SERVES 8

*2kg (4lb) unsmoked middle gammon joint • 2 onions, halved
about 35 whole cloves • 3 bay leaves
10 peppercorns • 600ml (1pt) dry cider*
FOR THE GLAZE
60g (2oz) butter • 4tbsp black treacle
FOR THE CRANBERRY SAUCE
*350g (11½oz) fresh or frozen cranberries • 175g (6oz) caster sugar
grated zest and juice of 2 clementines • 2tbsp Cointreau or
orange liqueur • 1tbsp redcurrant jelly*

1 Soak the gammon in cold water for about 6 hours, then drain. Place in a large pan with the onions, 5 cloves, the bay leaves and the peppercorns. Add the cider and enough water to cover the ham. Slowly bring to the boil. Cover and simmer for 2 hours. Preheat the oven to 220°C/425°F/Gas 7.

2 For the glaze, melt the butter and treacle in a pan. Drain the ham, peel off the skin and score the fat in a criss-cross pattern with a sharp knife. Place in a roasting tin and stud with the remaining cloves. Brush with the glaze, and bake for 25–30 minutes, or until crisp.

3 Meanwhile, bring all the ingredients for the cranberry sauce to the boil and simmer for 20 minutes, stirring occasionally. Serve the ham with the cranberry sauce.

BOEUF EN CROÛTE

THIS IS THE PERFECT DISH TO SERVE ON NEW YEAR'S
EVE – IT CAN BE MADE IN ADVANCE, IT LOOKS
SPECTACULAR AND TASTES DIVINE.

SERVES 8

*2tbsp olive oil • 1.5kg (3lb) whole fillet of beef
400g (13oz) ready-made puff pastry • beaten egg yolk, to glaze
flat-leaf parsley, to garnish*
FOR THE STUFFING
*30g (1oz) butter • 100g (3½oz) chestnut mushrooms, finely chopped
2 cloves garlic, crushed • 2tbsp chopped fresh parsley
salt and freshly ground black pepper*

1 Preheat the oven to 220°C/425°F/Gas 7. Heat the oil in a large frying pan. Add the meat and brown on all sides for about 10 minutes. Transfer to a roasting tin and bake for 20 minutes. Leave to cool.

2 For the stuffing, add the butter to the frying pan and heat until foaming. Add the mushrooms and garlic and cook for 5 minutes or until the mushrooms are soft. Remove from the heat and stir in the parsley and seasoning.

3 Roll the pastry out to a rectangle large enough to wrap around the beef. Spread the mushroom mixture down the centre of the pastry and set the beef on top.

4 Brush the edges of the pastry with beaten egg yolk. Fold the long pastry edges over the beef. Turn the beef over, transfer to a baking tray and tuck under the ends of the pastry. Brush liberally with beaten egg to glaze.

5 Bake in the hot oven for 30–40 minutes. Remove from the oven and leave to stand for 10 minutes. Garnish with flat-leaf parsley before serving.

THAI GREEN CURRY

SERVES 8

FOR THE CURRY PASTE

4 green chillies, halved and seeded • *2 stalks lemon grass, sliced*
3 shallots, peeled and halved • *4 cloves garlic*
1cm (½in) piece of galangal (Thai ginger) or fresh root ginger, peeled
grated zest of 1 lemon • *1tsp coriander seeds* • *1tsp ground cumin*
1tsp shrimp paste

TO COMPLETE

400ml (14fl oz) coconut milk • *8 chicken breasts, skinned and boned*
225g (7½oz) canned bamboo shoots • *2tbsp Thai fish sauce*
2tbsp muscovado sugar • *1 red and 1 green chilli, seeded*
and cut into strips • *2tbsp chopped fresh coriander leaves*

1 Blend all the paste ingredients together in a food processor until smooth. In a large frying pan, bring half the coconut milk to the boil, then simmer until reduced by half. Add the paste and simmer for a further 5 minutes.

2 Slice the chicken and add to the frying pan with the remaining coconut milk, bamboo shoots, fish sauce and muscovado sugar. Stir well and simmer for 10 minutes or until the chicken is tender. Garnish with strips of red and green chilli and chopped coriander. Serve with Turmeric Pilau Rice (*see page 106*).

BONED STUFFED TURKEY

DON'T JUST SERVE TURKEY AT CHRISTMAS – IT MAKES GOOD PARTY FARE ALL YEAR ROUND. TO MAKE CARVING EASY, ASK YOUR BUTCHER TO BONE THE TURKEY.

SERVES 8

5kg (11lb) turkey, breast bones removed, legs intact
salt and freshly ground black pepper • *30g (1oz) butter*

FOR THE STUFFING

1 large onion, chopped • *2tbsp olive oil*
225g (7½oz) rindless streaky bacon, chopped • *250g (8oz) fresh white*
breadcrumbs • *2tbsp chopped fresh thyme*
2tbsp chopped fresh parsley • *grated zest of 2 lemons*
1 medium egg, beaten

1 Preheat the oven to 190°C/375°F/Gas 5. Spread the turkey out on a work surface and season liberally with salt and freshly ground black pepper.

2 For the stuffing, fry the onion in the oil until softened but not coloured. Mix with all the remaining stuffing ingredients and pack neatly into the centre cavity of the bird. Using cocktail sticks and, if you have one, a trussing needle, carefully reshape the bird and tie securely.

3 Weigh the turkey and place it in a large roasting tin. Smear with the butter and season with plenty of salt and freshly ground black pepper. Cover with a sheet of buttered foil. Roast the turkey for about 4½ hours – allowing 25 minutes per 500g (1lb) plus 25 minutes – or until the juices from the thickest part of the thigh run clear when pierced with a skewer. Remove the foil for the last 25 minutes of the cooking time to allow the turkey to brown.

4 Remove the bird from the oven, cover tightly with foil and leave to stand for 15 minutes to make carving easier or, if serving cold, leave to cool completely.

VARIATION

If you would rather not bone and stuff the turkey, fill its cavity with onions, halved lemons and a small bunch of thyme. Cook as above. Shape the stuffing into small balls and cook around the turkey for the last 25 minutes of the cooking time.

Vegetables & Salads

ATTRACTIVE, NUTRITIOUS AND DELICIOUS, VEGETABLES LIE AT THE HEART OF ANY SUCCESSFUL PARTY MEAL. ENRICH YOUR MENUS WITH AN INSPIRATIONAL MIX OF THESE DELICIOUS MAIN COURSE VEGETABLE DISHES AND ACCOMPANIMENTS.

Tuscan Bean Salad

TO SAVE TIME SOAKING AND COOKING DRIED BEANS, BUY THE CANNED VARIETIES. THIS SALAD CAN ALSO BE SERVED WARMED WITH SMOKED SAUSAGE AS A QUICK SUPPER–PARTY DISH.

SERVES 8

400g (13oz) canned cannellini beans, rinsed and drained
400g (13oz) canned flageolet beans, rinsed and drained
400g (13oz) canned black-eyed beans, rinsed and drained
150g (5oz) canned black olives • small basil leaves, to garnish

FOR THE DRESSING

1tbsp red wine vinegar • 90ml (3fl oz) extra-virgin olive oil
2tbsp Parmesan, grated • small bunch basil
salt and freshly ground black pepper

1 In one large serving bowl or several smaller ones – depending on table size and location – mix together the drained beans and olives.

2 For the dressing, blend the vinegar, oil and Parmesan in a food processor. Add the leaves from the basil and whiz again. Season with salt and pepper to taste.

3 Drizzle the dressing over the beans and olives and toss to combine. Scatter with small basil leaves just before serving.

Minted Potato Salad

SERVED HOT OR COLD, THIS SALAD IS AN IDEAL ACCOMPANIMENT TO LAMB AND CHICKEN DISHES.

SERVES 8

1kg (2lb) baby new potatoes • 2 sprigs mint
FOR THE DRESSING
4tbsp mayonnaise • 4tbsp natural yogurt
3tbsp chopped fresh mint leaves • 2tbsp capers, rinsed and drained
salt and freshly ground black pepper

1 Put the potatoes in a saucepan and cover with cold water. Add a little salt and the sprigs of mint. Bring to the boil, then simmer for 12–15 minutes or until the potatoes are cooked. Drain, and discard the mint.

2 Meanwhile, blend the dressing ingredients in a food processor. Once smooth, season with salt and pepper.

3 Toss the warm potatoes in the dressing. Serve warm or leave to cool, as preferred.

Rocket Salad

SERVES 6

250g (8oz) rocket leaves • 3tbsp walnut oil
2tbsp olive oil • 2tbsp red wine vinegar
2tsp grainy mustard • ½tsp caster sugar
125g (4oz) walnut halves

Place the rocket leaves in a bowl. Whisk the oils, vinegar, mustard and sugar together to make a dressing, then toss with the leaves. Serve sprinkled with the walnut halves.

ANTIPASTO PASTA SALAD

SERVES 4

225g (7½oz) pasta twists • 275g (9oz) roasted peppers in oil, drained
100g (3½oz) pitted black olives • 4 sundried tomatoes, quartered
100g (3½oz) Roquefort cheese, crumbled • 10 slices peppered salami
100g (3½oz) mixed leaf salad

FOR THE DRESSING
4tbsp oil from the peppers • 4tbsp white wine vinegar
2tbsp chopped fresh oregano • 2 cloves garlic, crushed
salt and freshly ground black pepper

1 Cook the pasta in a large pan of boiling salted water, according to the packet instructions. Drain, then rinse with cold water.

2 Cut the peppers into long, fine strips. Mix together the peppers, olives, tomatoes and cheese. Stir in the pasta and peppered salami and mix well.

3 Divide the salad leaves between four glass bowls and spoon the pasta salad over them. Whisk together all the ingredients for the dressing and divide between the bowls. Serve at once.

PESTO COUSCOUS SALAD

THIS SALAD CAN BE MADE QUICKLY
USING STORECUPBOARD INGREDIENTS.

SERVES 8

450g (1lb) instant couscous • 125g (4oz) fresh pesto
125g (4oz) sundried peppers in oil, drained and sliced
125g (4oz) chargrilled aubergines in oil, drained and sliced
salt and freshly ground black pepper • basil leaves, to garnish

1 Put the couscous in a heatproof bowl. Cover with boiling water and leave to stand for 5 minutes, or until the liquid has been absorbed and the couscous is tender.

2 Stir the pesto into the couscous to colour it evenly. Fold in the peppers and aubergines, then season with salt and black pepper to taste. Spoon into a serving dish and garnish with basil leaves just before serving.

STIR-FRIED GREEN VEGETABLES

SERVES 6

2tbsp groundnut oil • 3 spring onions, trimmed and quartered
1 green pepper, seeded and thinly sliced • 125g (4oz) Savoy cabbage,
thinly shredded • 125g (4oz) mangetout, trimmed and halved
60g (2oz) beansprouts • 1tbsp Thai green curry paste

1 Heat the groundnut oil in a wok or large frying pan until very hot. Add the spring onions and green pepper and stir-fry for about 3 minutes. Add the cabbage and mangetout and stir for another 2 minutes.

2 Stir in the beansprouts, then add the Thai green curry paste. Continue to stir until the sauce starts to bubble and the vegetables are well flavoured. Serve immediately.

CHICKPEA DHAL

SERVE THIS DISH WITH CURRIES AND OTHER SPICY FOOD. AS AN ALTERNATIVE TO CHICKPEAS, USE YELLOW OR ORANGE SPLIT PEAS, COOKED ACCORDING TO PACKET INSTRUCTIONS.

SERVES 8

2tbsp sunflower oil or ghee • 1 medium onion, finely chopped
1tsp coriander seeds • 1tsp garam masala • 1tsp turmeric
large pinch of hot chilli powder • large pinch of salt
800g (1¾lb) cooked chickpeas • 2tbsp chopped fresh coriander

1 Heat the oil or ghee in a large pan, add the onion and cook for about 3 minutes. Add the spices and salt to the pan and cook, stirring constantly, for 1–2 minutes, until the spices begin to release their aromas.

2 Stir the chickpeas into the pan and cook for a further 5 minutes. Garnish with the chopped coriander before serving.

TURMERIC PILAU RICE

PILAU RICE LITERALLY MEANS PORRIDGE RICE BUT HERE THE LONG-GRAIN RICE COOKED IN A FLAVOURED STOCK IS FIT FOR THE FINEST BANQUET. TURMERIC TURNS THE RICE A WARM, DELICATE YELLOW.

SERVES 8

2tbsp sunflower oil • 1 medium onion, finely chopped
2 cloves garlic, finely chopped • 2tsp turmeric • 1tsp ground ginger
1tsp ground coriander • ½tsp salt • 750ml (1¼pt) vegetable stock
500g (1lb) long-grain rice • coriander leaves, to garnish

1 Heat the oil in a large, lidded saucepan, add the onion and garlic and cook for 2 minutes. Add the turmeric, ginger, coriander and salt and cook for a further 2 minutes, stirring constantly. Pour the stock into the pan and bring to the boil.

2 Add the rice to the pan. Cover the pan with a lid and simmer for 15 minutes, or until the rice is tender and the liquid has been absorbed. Serve in a warm dish, garnished with coriander leaves.

POMMES DAUPHINOIS

SERVES 8

melted butter, to grease dish
1kg (2lb) waxy potatoes, peeled and thinly sliced
2 medium onions, thinly sliced • 60g (2oz) butter, cubed
salt and freshly ground black pepper • 300ml (½pt) double cream
2 cloves garlic, peeled • 60g (2oz) Parmesan, grated
1tbsp snipped chives, to garnish

1 Preheat the oven to 180°C/350°F/Gas 4. Brush a large shallow ovenproof dish with a little melted butter.

2 Put the potatoes in a saucepan, cover with water and bring to the boil. Simmer for 3 minutes, then drain.

3 When the potatoes have cooled, arrange a layer in the base of the prepared dish. Cover with a layer of onion then top with some butter cubes and seasoning. Repeat this layering sequence until all the ingredients have been used.

4 Meanwhile, heat the cream with the garlic. When steaming, remove it from the heat and strain over the potatoes. Sprinkle with Parmesan. Bake for 1¼ hours, until lightly coloured. Serve garnished with the snipped chives.

CHEESY JACKET POTATOES

MAKES 6

6 medium baking potatoes • 3tbsp extra-virgin olive oil
coarse sea salt, for sprinkling • a few sprigs thyme
FOR THE TOPPING
90g (3oz) Gruyère cheese, grated • 90g (3oz) Red Leicester cheese, grated
salt and freshly ground black pepper • 2tsp powdered mustard

1 Preheat the oven to 180°C/350°F/Gas 4. Lightly prick the skins of the potatoes, then arrange in a roasting tin. Drizzle over the olive oil, sprinkle with sea salt and scatter with thyme sprigs. Bake for 1 hour or until the potatoes are soft on the inside.

2 Remove from the oven, halve, and scoop out the flesh. Mix the flesh with the grated cheese, season with salt and pepper, and the mustard to taste. Return the potato to the skins and, if necessary, reheat before serving.

ROAST SWEET POTATOES

THESE BRIGHT ORANGE POTATOES MAKE A
DELICIOUS ALTERNATIVE TO ORDINARY ROAST POTATOES.
SERVE WITH ANY ROASTED MEAT.

SERVES 8

500g (1lb) sweet potatoes • 1tsp salt • 90g (3oz) white vegetable fat
a few sprigs rosemary

1 Preheat the oven to 220°C/425°F/Gas 7. Peel the
potatoes and cut into even-sized pieces. Place them
in a saucepan, cover with water and add the salt. Bring
to the boil and cook for about 5 minutes. Drain the
water from the pan and shake the pan to roughen the
potatoes slightly.

2 Put the vegetable fat in a roasting tin and heat in
the oven or on the hob until it melts and begins to
bubble. Carefully add the potatoes and roast in the oven
for about 50 minutes. Turn the potatoes occasionally
to make sure they brown and crisp evenly and, after
40 minutes, add the rosemary sprigs.

COURGETTES WITH GARLIC

YOU CAN ALSO TRY THIS RECIPE USING CARROTS, BRUSSELS
SPROUTS, TURNIPS OR SWEDES INSTEAD OF COURGETTES,
OR USE A SELECTION TO MAKE A TASTY VEGETABLE MEDLEY.

SERVES 8

90g (3oz) butter • 1–2 cloves garlic, very thinly sliced
juice and zest of 1 small lime
750g (1½lb) small courgettes, halved and trimmed into barrel shapes
salt and freshly ground black pepper • 2tbsp chopped fresh parsley

1 Melt the butter in a pan, add the garlic and cook for
2 minutes. Add the lime zest and juice and, when
bubbling, add the courgettes and cook for 3–4 minutes
or until tender.

2 Season with salt and freshly ground black pepper to
taste and serve sprinkled with the chopped parsley.

FESTIVE FILO PIE

THIS RICHLY FLAVOURED DISH MAKES HEARTY
CHRISTMAS FARE, SERVED EITHER COLD AT A BUFFET
LUNCH OR PIPING HOT AT A FESTIVE SUPPER.

SERVES 8

FOR THE FILLING
2 yellow peppers • 2 green peppers • 2 red peppers
30g (1oz) butter • 2 medium leeks, trimmed and sliced
300g (10oz) chestnut mushrooms, trimmed and sliced
2 cloves garlic, chopped • 250g (8oz) Gruyère cheese, thinly sliced
2tbsp chopped fresh parsley • salt and freshly ground black pepper
FOR THE PASTRY
300g (10oz) filo pastry, thawed if frozen • 30g (1oz) butter, melted
TO GARNISH
½ each yellow, green and red pepper

1 Preheat the oven to 200°C/400°F/Gas 6. Arrange all the
peppers on the tray of a grill pan and cook under
a hot grill, turning occasionally until the skins blacken on
all sides. Carefully transfer the peppers to polythene bags,
tie, and leave to cool. Take the peppers from the bags and
peel, core, seed and quarter them.

2 Melt the butter in a pan and cook the leeks for about
5 minutes, until softened. Remove from the pan and
set aside. Add the sliced mushrooms and garlic and cook
for a further 5 minutes or until the liquid has evaporated.

3 Use two thirds of the filo pastry to line a 25cm (10in)
round spring-clip tin or a 1kg (2lb) drop-sided terrine
tin. Brush the pastry with melted butter.

4 Layer the peppers, leeks, mushrooms and cheese in
the pastry case, sprinkling each layer with parsley,
salt and pepper.

5 Cover the top of the pie with strips of the remaining
filo and brush with a little more melted butter. Bake
the pie for about 20 minutes or until golden. Remove the
sides of the tin and return the pie to the oven briefly to
brown the sides lightly.

6 Meanwhile, prepare the pepper halves for the garnish
as in step 1. Cut holly leaf shapes from the peppers
and use to garnish the pie before serving.

DESSERTS & CAKES

THESE DELICIOUS CONFECTIONS INEVITABLY TAKE MORE TIME TO CREATE THAN THE OTHER RECIPES IN THE BOOK BUT NO PARTY IS COMPLETE WITHOUT A SPECIAL CAKE OR DESSERT. THE TRICK IS TO MAKE THEM IN ADVANCE.

HAZELNUT MERINGUE GÂTEAU

THIS MERINGUE GÂTEAU CAN BE MADE GHOST–SHAPED FOR A HALLOWE'EN PARTY. CREATE THE GHOST'S EYES AND MOUTH FROM LIQUORICE OR BLACK–TINTED ICING.

MAKES ONE 20CM (8IN) GÂTEAU

4 medium egg whites • *250g (8oz) caster sugar*
125g (4oz) hazelnuts, toasted and chopped
TO COMPLETE
3tbsp granulated sugar • *12 hazelnuts* • *300ml (½pt) double cream*
2tbsp icing sugar • *2tbsp strong black coffee*
sifted icing sugar • *sifted cocoa powder*

1 Preheat the oven to 110°C/225°F/Gas ¼. Line three baking sheets with baking parchment, each marked with a 20cm (8in) circle, or ghost shape.

2 Whisk the egg whites with an electric whisk until stiff but not dry. With the whisk running, add the sugar a tablespoon at a time, making sure the mixture is stiff before adding more sugar. When all the sugar has been added the mixture will be stiff and glossy. Fold in the hazelnuts.

3 Divide the mixture between the marked shapes and spread flat. Bake for about 3 hours, or until the meringues are crisp and dry. Leave to cool.

4 Heat the granulated sugar in a pan with 1 tablespoon water, until it has dissolved and browned. Add the hazelnuts and stir to coat evenly. Transfer the coated hazelnuts to a lightly oiled surface and leave to cool.

5 Lightly whip the cream with the icing sugar and coffee. Use the flavoured cream to sandwich the meringues together. Arrange the caramel-coated hazelnuts on top. Serve dusted with icing sugar and cocoa.

CHOCOLATE TART

SERVES 8

FOR THE PASTRY
250g (8oz) plain flour • *125g (4oz) butter, diced*
60g (2oz) icing sugar, sifted • *1 medium egg, beaten*
FOR THE FILLING
300g (10oz) plain chocolate, chopped • *150g (5oz) unsalted butter*
180ml (6fl oz) double cream
TO SERVE
sifted icing sugar • *sifted cocoa powder*
150ml (¼pt) double cream, lightly whipped

1 Sift the flour into a bowl, then rub in the butter until the flour has the texture of coarse breadcrumbs. Mix in the icing sugar, then stir in the egg and add a little iced water, if necessary, to form a soft but not sticky pastry. Cover and chill for about 15 minutes.

2 Preheat the oven to 190°C/375°F/Gas 5. Roll out the pastry on a lightly floured surface and use it to line a 25cm (10in) tart tin. Prick the base and chill for 15 minutes. Line the pastry case with scrunched foil and bake for 10 minutes. Discard the foil and return the pastry to the oven for a further 5 minutes.

3 Meanwhile, prepare the filling. Put the chopped chocolate, butter and cream in a heatproof bowl. Set the bowl over a pan of simmering water. Heat the mixture until the chocolate melts, stirring frequently to ensure the ingredients blend together.

4 Remove the bowl from the heat and stir the mixture until it begins to cool and thicken. Pour the mixture into the baked pastry case and leave until set. Serve sprinkled with sifted icing sugar and cocoa powder. Accompany each slice of tart with a little whipped cream.

CHOCOLATE ROULADE

THE MARVELLOUS THING ABOUT THIS RICH DESSERT
IS THAT IT CAN BE MADE, FILLED AND FROZEN FOR
UP TO A MONTH BEFORE SERVING.

SERVES 8

FOR THE SPONGE

4 medium eggs, separated • 150g (5oz) caster sugar
15g (½oz) plain flour, sifted • 15g (½oz) cocoa powder, sifted
75g (2½oz) plain chocolate, melted
sifted icing sugar

FOR THE FILLING

450ml (¾pt) double cream • 75g (2½oz) plain chocolate, melted

1 Preheat the oven to 180°C/350°F/Gas 4. Grease and line a Swiss roll tin measuring 20cm x 30cm (8in x 12in). Whisk the egg yolks and half the sugar with an electric whisk until pale and thick, about 5 minutes. Fold in the flour, cocoa powder and melted chocolate.

2 Whisk the egg whites until stiff, gradually adding the remaining sugar. Fold the sugared egg whites into the chocolate mixture. Spread the cake mixture into the prepared tin and bake for 20 minutes or until well risen and springy to the touch. Cover with a damp tea towel, then leave to cool.

3 Turn the sponge out on to a sheet of greaseproof paper dusted with icing sugar. For the filling, stir 150ml (¼pt) of the double cream into the melted chocolate and whisk until thick. Spread the chocolate mixture over the roulade. Whip the remaining cream and spread it over the chocolate mixture.

4 Use the greaseproof paper to help you roll up the roulade. The roulade will crack as it rolls. Cover and chill for up to 12 hours before serving, or freeze for up to one month.

RICH CHOCOLATE CHEESECAKE

SERVES 8

400g (13oz) plain chocolate digestive biscuits
100g (3½oz) butter • sifted icing sugar

FOR THE FILLING

250g (8oz) plain chocolate • 150ml (¼pt) soured cream
3 medium eggs • 125g (4oz) caster sugar
625g (1¼lb) full-fat cream cheese, softened

1 Preheat the oven to 180°C/350°F/Gas 4. Finely crush the chocolate biscuits in a food processor. Melt the butter in a pan and stir in the crushed biscuits. Spoon the biscuit mixture into a 23cm (9in) spring-clip tin and press down over the base. Chill while preparing the filling.

2 Break the chocolate into pieces and melt in a bowl placed over a pan of simmering water. Remove from the heat and stir in the soured cream. Whisk the eggs and sugar until pale and thick. Blend in the softened cream cheese, then fold in the chocolate mixture.

3 Pour the mixture over the biscuit layer and bake for 1½ hours or until firm to the touch. Leave to cool in the tin. Unclip the tin and transfer the cheesecake to a flat serving plate. Sprinkle liberally with sifted icing sugar.

TIRAMISU

SERVES 4

125g (4oz) ratafia biscuits • 60ml (4tbsp) strong black coffee
60ml (4tbsp) coffee liqueur • 300ml (½pt) ready-made custard
250g (8oz) mascarpone cheese
300ml (½pt) double cream, lightly whipped • sifted cocoa powder

1 Divide the biscuits between four glass dishes. Pour the black coffee and coffee liqueur over the biscuits.

2 Pour over a layer of custard. Beat together the mascarpone and cream and spoon it over the custard. Smooth the surface and chill for at least one hour. Serve dusted with cocoa powder.

Mini Baked Alaska

This great dessert can be prepared well in advance. Add the meringue and bake just before serving.

Serves 8

For the Sponge

3 medium eggs • *75g (2½oz) caster sugar*
60g (2oz) plain flour, sifted • *1tbsp cocoa powder, sifted*

For the Ice Cream

60g (2oz) sultanas • *90ml (3fl oz) brandy*
400ml (14fl oz) fresh custard • *600ml (1pt) double cream*

For the Meringue

6 medium egg whites • *350g (11½oz) caster sugar*

1 To make the sponge base, first preheat the oven to 190°C/375°F/Gas 5. Grease and line a Swiss roll tin measuring 20cm x 30cm (8in x 12in). Use an electric whisk to whisk the eggs with the sugar until thick and pale, about 5 minutes.

2 Sift the flour and cocoa powder together and carefully fold into the egg mixture. Pour into the prepared tin and bake for about 12 minutes or until risen. Turn out on to a wire rack and leave to cool. Cut out 8 rounds using a 7.5cm (3in) diameter ramekin.

3 For the ice cream, put the sultanas into a bowl and pour over the brandy. Leave to stand for about 1 hour. Meanwhile, stir the custard and double cream together, then freeze until firm. Fold the sultanas and brandy into the custard mixture, and freeze until solid, about 2 hours.

4 Preheat the oven to 220°C/425°F/Gas 7. Place the sponge rounds on a large baking tray and set a large scoop of the ice cream on top of each one. Put the tray in the freezer while preparing the meringue.

5 Whisk the egg whites until stiff. Gradually whisk in the caster sugar. Swirl or pipe the meringue on to the ice cream and sponge, covering them completely. Bake for 5–7 minutes, then serve immediately.

Variation

Mincemeat Christmas Bombe: In step 3, stir 125g (4oz) vegetarian mincemeat and 2 tablespoons brandy into the ice cream mixture and freeze in a 1 litre (1¾pt) mould, lined with clingfilm. Follow the recipe as instructed.

Plum Pudding

Serves 8

250g (8oz) stoned prunes, chopped • *250g (8oz) raisins*
250g (8oz) sultanas • *275ml (9fl oz) brown ale*
2tbsp black treacle • *75g (2½oz) plain flour* • *1tsp ground mixed spice*
175g (6oz) shredded vegetarian suet • *175g (6oz) white breadcrumbs*
250g (8oz) unrefined molasses sugar • *60g (2oz) flaked almonds*
1 apple, cored and grated • *grated rind and juice of 1 orange*
2 medium eggs, beaten

To Complete

4tbsp brandy • *sifted icing sugar* • *holly sprig*
brandy butter and cream, to serve

1 Put the dried fruit in a bowl, pour over the brown ale, then stir in the black treacle. Cover the bowl with clingfilm and leave to stand overnight.

2 Mix the flour, mixed spice, suet, breadcrumbs, sugar, almonds and apple. Tip the fruit mixture into the flour, with the orange rind and juice and the eggs then mix well.

3 Spoon the mixture into a greased 2 litre (3pt) pudding basin. Cover with greased greaseproof paper and foil, then tie securely with string.

4 Place the pudding in a lidded pan containing 2.5cm (1in) boiling water and steam for 6 hours, topping up with boiling water as necessary. Leave to cool, then wrap in fresh greaseproof paper.

5 Before serving, wrap sterilized, heatproof charms in greaseproof paper and insert into the pudding, if desired. Re-cover and steam for a further 4 hours before turning out on to a warmed serving plate.

6 To flame the pudding, pour a little warmed brandy around the base of the pudding, dust with icing sugar, decorate with holly, and light with a match. Serve with brandy butter (*see below*) and cream.

Brandy Butter

175g (6oz) butter, softened • *175g (6oz) icing sugar, sifted*
2tbsp brandy

Beat together the softened butter and the icing sugar until pale and light. Gradually blend in the brandy. Spoon into a serving dish, cover and chill until ready to serve.

POACHED PEACHES

STORED IN AIRTIGHT JARS, POACHED PEACHES MAKE
AN IDEAL DESSERT FOR SMART PICNICS.

MAKES ONE JAR

1 bottle dessert wine • 60g (2oz) caster sugar
thinly grated zest of 1 orange • 3 whole cloves
1 cinnamon stick, halved • 8 ripe but firm peaches

1 Pour the wine into a shallow pan, then add the sugar,
orange zest, cloves and cinnamon. Heat gently until
the sugar has dissolved, then add 150ml (¼pt) water.

2 Add the peaches to the pan and cover with a disc of
baking parchment. Cook gently for about 30 minutes,
or until the peaches are tender.

3 Carefully transfer the peaches to a sterilized, sealable
jar and cover with the liquid. Seal and leave to cool.

PEACH MELBA TRIFLE

SERVES 8

250g (8oz) ratafia biscuits • 6 peaches, peeled, stoned and sliced
250g (8oz) raspberries • 150ml (¼pt) medium dry sherry
400g (13oz) ready-made custard

FOR THE TOPPING

600ml (1pt) double cream • grated zest of 1 orange
90ml (3fl oz) brandy • 30g (1oz) caster sugar
30g (1oz) flaked almonds, toasted

1 Break the ratafias up and place them in a large glass
bowl. Arrange the sliced peaches on top. Sprinkle the
raspberries over the peaches and add the sherry. Cover
and leave for at least 3 hours.

2 Spoon the custard over the fruit mixture. Whisk
the cream, orange zest, brandy and sugar until stiff.
Spoon on to the custard, then cover and chill for up to
12 hours. Scatter with the almonds just before serving.

VARIATION

WINTER TRIFLE: Replace the peaches with 250g (8oz) dried
apricots that have been soaked in 150ml (¼pt) brandy. Omit
the sherry and raspberries. Melt 100g (3½oz) strawberry
jam and pour it over the apricots. Continue as instructed.

RICOTTA TART WITH SEASONAL FRUIT

THIS CLASSIC ITALIAN TART IS IDEAL TO SERVE AT PICNICS OR BUFFET PARTIES WITH FRESH FIGS OR SEASONAL FRUIT.

SERVES 8

1 quantity Pastry (see Chocolate Tart, page 108)
3 fresh figs, quartered, or seasonal fruit, to decorate
FOR THE FILLING
500g (1lb) ricotta cheese • 4 medium eggs, separated
100g (3½oz) caster sugar • grated zest of 1 lemon
175g (6oz) luxury dried fruits such as cranberries,
mangoes or peaches, chopped • 2tbsp plain flour

1 Preheat the oven to 190°C/375°F/Gas 5. Roll out the pastry on a lightly floured work surface and use it to line a 20cm (8in), deep fluted flan tin. Line with scrunched foil and bake blind for 10 minutes. Remove the foil and return to the oven for a further 10 minutes.

2 For the filling, beat together the ricotta, egg yolks, sugar, lemon zest, dried fruit and flour. Whisk the egg whites until stiff, and fold them in with a large metal spoon. Spoon the mixture into the pastry case and bake for 1 hour or until golden and set. Cool before serving.

VARIATIONS

TARTE AU CITRON: Prepare and bake the pastry case as above. Stir together 250g (8oz) sugar and 2 tablespoons cornflour in a heatproof bowl. Gradually mix in the grated zest and juice of 2 lemons and 100g (3½oz) butter.

★ Set the bowl over a pan of simmering water and stir until the butter and sugar have melted. When the mixture begins to thicken remove it from the heat.

★ Beat 3 medium eggs into the mixture and return it to the heat for 3 minutes. Pour the lemon mixture into the pastry case. Bake at 190°C/375°F/Gas 5 for 20 minutes or until the lemon custard has almost set.

★ Leave to cool in the tin for about 10 minutes before transferring to a serving plate. Serve dusted with icing sugar and decorated with a few raspberries.

PECAN PIES: Line the 20cm (8in) flan tin or six individual 10cm (4in) tins and bake blind as instructed above.

★ Divide 400g (13oz) pecan nuts between the pastry cases.
★ Mix together 30g (1oz) melted butter, 175g (6oz) soft light-brown sugar, 4 medium eggs, 175ml (6fl oz) golden syrup and 30g (1oz) plain flour. Pour into the prepared pastry cases and bake for 45 or 30 minutes respectively.

SUMMER BERRY TARTS

MAKES 16

1 quantity Pastry (see Chocolate Tart, page 108)
CRÈME PATISSIÈRE
3 medium egg yolks • 100g (3½oz) caster sugar • 2tbsp cornflour
300ml (½pt) milk
FOR THE TOPPING
450g (14½oz) mixed summer berries, such as strawberries, redcurrants,
blueberries and raspberries • 4tbsp redcurrant jelly

1 Preheat the oven to 190°C/375°F/Gas 5. Divide the pastry into 16 pieces. Roll out the pieces on a lightly floured surface and use them to line individual tartlet or patty tins. Prick the bases and chill for 10 minutes. Line each with foil and bake blind for 5 minutes. Remove the foil and return to the oven for a further 5 minutes.

2 For the crème patissière, whisk together the egg yolks, caster sugar and cornflour with 2 tablespoons milk. Heat the remaining milk until it begins to bubble, then pour it into the egg mixture, whisking continuously.

3 Rinse out the pan and return the mixture to it. Reheat, stirring occasionally, until the mixture boils and thickens. Whisk until thick and smooth. Leave to cool, covered with wetted greaseproof paper.

4 Spoon the crème patissière into the cooled pastry cases. Just before serving, top the tartlets with the berries and brush with warmed redcurrant jelly to glaze.

TROPICAL FRUIT SALAD

SERVES 8

3 small pineapples • 2 mangoes • 2 kiwi fruit • 2 pawpaws
zest and juice of 2 oranges and 1 lime • 150g (5oz) caster sugar

1 Trim and peel the pineapples and cut the flesh into wedges. Peel, stone and slice the mangoes, and peel and slice the kiwi fruit. Peel the pawpaws, discard the seeds, then cut them into slices. Mix all the fruit in a bowl.

2 Heat the juice of the oranges and the lime with the caster sugar. Once the sugar has dissolved, bring the mixture to the boil, then simmer for 5 minutes. Stir in the zest of one of the oranges and half the lime. Pour the syrup over the fruit and mix well. Chill, then serve.

COCONUT ICE CREAM

SERVED WITH A TROPICAL FRUIT SALAD, THIS DELICATELY
FLAVOURED COCONUT ICE CREAM IS THE PERFECT
DESSERT TO COMPLEMENT SPICY FOOD.

SERVES 8

300ml (½pt) milk • 150ml (¼pt) coconut milk
4 green cardamom pods, crushed • 2 strips lemon zest
4 medium egg yolks • 125g (4oz) caster sugar • 1tbsp cornflour
200ml (7fl oz) double cream, lightly whipped

1 Heat the milk with the coconut milk, cardamom pods and lemon zest until it just begins to steam. Meanwhile, whisk the egg yolks with the caster sugar and cornflour until pale and light.

2 Pour the warm milk into the egg mixture and whisk together to form a custard. Rinse the pan, add the custard and continue heating until it begins to thicken and bubble. Remove from the heat and allow to cool.

3 Strain the custard and fold in the double cream. Freeze in a container for 2 hours or until slushy. Whisk until smooth and return to the freezer for a further 2 hours. Whisk again, then freeze until solid.

4 Leave the ice cream to stand for about 10 minutes at room temperature before serving with Tropical Fruit Salad (*see above*).

BLUEBERRY MUFFINS

MAKES 12 LARGE OR 24 SMALL MUFFINS

175g (6oz) plain flour • 75g (2½oz) golden caster sugar
1tbsp baking powder • 1tsp ground cinnamon • ½tsp salt
150g (5oz) fresh blueberries • 175ml (6fl oz) buttermilk
1 medium egg, beaten • 125g (4oz) butter, melted

1 Preheat the oven to 220°C/425°F/Gas 7. Line muffin tins with paper cases.

2 Sift together the flour, sugar, baking powder, cinnamon and salt. Stir in the blueberries.

3 Whisk together the buttermilk, egg and melted butter. Gradually work the liquid into the flour mixture. Spoon into the paper cases and bake for about 8–15 minutes, depending on size, or until well risen.

BONFIRE CAKES

MAKES 16

175g (6oz) butter, softened • 175g (6oz) golden caster sugar
3 medium eggs, beaten • 175g (6oz) self-raising flour
125g (4oz) raspberry jam
TO DECORATE
125g (4oz) unsalted butter, softened • 200g (7oz) icing sugar, sifted
125g (4oz) plain chocolate, melted

1 Preheat the oven to 190°C/375°F/Gas 5. Line a patty tin with paper cases.

2 Cream the butter and sugar until pale and light. Gradually beat in the eggs, then sift the flour over the creamed mixture and fold in.

3 Spoon the cake mixture into the paper cases to half fill them. Put a little raspberry jam on top before adding the remaining cake mixture. Bake for 15–20 minutes or until risen. Leave to cool, then remove the paper cases.

4 To make the decoration, beat the butter with the icing sugar and half the melted chocolate. Spread the remaining chocolate on to a clean flat surface and leave until just set. Use a knife to make chocolate curls.

5 Turn the cakes upside down and spread over the chocolate icing. Arrange the chocolate curls on the top and sides to resemble twigs and branches on a bonfire.

GINGERBREAD

CUT OUT BEAR SHAPES FOR CHILDREN'S PARTIES AND DECORATE WITH FACES OR USE CHRISTMAS-SHAPED CUTTERS TO MAKE TREE DECORATIONS.

MAKES 15

60g (2oz) butter, softened • 125g (4oz) golden caster sugar
3tbsp black treacle • 1tbsp golden syrup
1 piece stem ginger, chopped • 4tbsp warm water
350g (11½oz) self-raising flour • 2tsp ground ginger
½tsp ground cinnamon
TO DECORATE
icing sugar • food colourings (optional)

1 Preheat the oven to 180°C/350°F/Gas 4. Grease 2 baking sheets with a little butter.

2 Cream the butter and sugar until pale and light. Beat in the black treacle, golden syrup and chopped ginger, then stir in the warm water.

3 Sift the flour, ground ginger and cinnamon into the creamed mixture, then mix to form a soft dough.

4 Knead on a floured surface and roll out thinly. Cut out 15 shapes and arrange on the baking sheets. Use a skewer to make small holes for stringing, if desired. Bake for 8–10 minutes, until golden. Leave to cool for 3 minutes before transferring to a wire rack to cool completely.

5 Sift some icing sugar into a small bowl. Add a few drops of water, and food colouring if using, to give a smooth consistency. Use a paper icing bag to pipe on decorations. Leave to set.

ICED FANCIES

DECORATE THESE DELICIOUSLY LIGHT CAKES WITH
CRYSTALLIZED EDIBLE FLOWERS OR FRUIT PEEL.

MAKES 15

250g (8oz) butter, softened • 300g (10oz) caster sugar
grated zest of 1 lemon and 1 small orange • 4 medium eggs, beaten
300g (10oz) self-raising flour • 60g (2oz) cornflour
3tbsp milk
TO DECORATE
6tbsp apricot jam, sieved and warmed • 750g (1½lb) white marzipan
1kg (2lb) ready-to-roll icing • food colouring (optional)
crystallized flowers • crystallized fruit peel

1 Preheat the oven to 180°C/350°F/Gas 4. Butter and
line a 30cm x 20cm (12in x 8in) cake tin.

2 Cream the butter with the sugar and grated zest until
pale and light. Gradually beat in the eggs. Sift the
flour and cornflour over the cake mixture and fold in
until just mixed. Add the milk and stir until smooth.

3 Spoon the mixture into the cake tin and bake for
about 50 minutes or until well risen and golden.
Turn out on to a wire rack and leave to cool.

4 Cut the cake into 15 shapes (circles, ovals, squares or
triangles). Brush the sides and tops of the mini cakes
with the warmed apricot jam. Roll out the marzipan and
use it to cover the cakes. Leave to dry for about 1 hour.
Colour the icing, if desired, roll it out and use to cover the
cakes. Decorate with the crystallized flowers and fruit peel.

MINI MERINGUES

MERINGUES CAN BE MADE IN A VARIETY OF SHAPES
FOR THEMED PARTIES, SUCH AS SNOWMEN AT
CHRISTMAS OR GHOSTS FOR HALLOWE'EN. THE
MERINGUES CAN BE MADE UP TO TWO WEEKS AHEAD
AND FILLED AN HOUR BEFORE SERVING.

MAKES ABOUT 20

3 medium egg whites • 175g (6oz) caster sugar
FOR THE FILLING
150ml (¼pt) double cream • 1tbsp caster sugar • ½tsp vanilla extract

1 Preheat the oven to 110°C/225°F/Gas¼. Line 2 baking
sheets with baking parchment. If making snowmen or
ghosts, draw the shapes on the underside of the parchment.

2 Using an electric whisk, whisk the egg whites until
stiff. With the whisk running, add the sugar,
1 tablespoon at a time, making sure the mixture has
thickened before adding more. The mixture should be
stiff and glossy.

3 Spoon the mixture into a piping bag fitted with a star
or plain nozzle. Pipe the mixture into the desired
shapes. Bake for 2 hours or until the meringues are crisp
and dry, then leave to cool.

4 For the filling, lightly whip the cream with the sugar
and vanilla extract. Use the flavoured cream to
sandwich the meringues together.

SIMPLE FAIRY CAKES

MAKES 15

100g (3½oz) butter, softened • 100g (3½oz) caster sugar
2 medium eggs • 100g (3½oz) self-raising flour

1 Preheat the oven to 190°C/375°F/Gas 5. Cream the
butter and sugar together until pale and light. Beat
in the eggs, then sift over the flour and fold in.

2 Divide the mixture between 15 bun tins lined with
paper cases. Bake for 15 minutes or until golden and
risen. Leave to cool, then remove the paper cases, and ice
with glacé icing (*see Gingerbread, opposite*) if wished.

TRIPLE CHOC COOKIES

MAKES 20

100g (3½oz) each white, plain and milk chocolate
60g (2oz) pecan nuts, roughly chopped • 100g (3½oz) butter, softened
100g (3½oz) soft light-brown sugar • 1 medium egg, beaten
225g (7½oz) plain flour • ½ tsp baking powder

1 Preheat the oven to 180°C/350°F/Gas 4. Chop the chocolate into chunks. Mix with the chopped pecans.

2 Beat the butter and sugar until light and fluffy, then gradually beat in the egg. Sift in the flour and baking powder and fold into the creamed mixture using a large metal spoon. Stir in the chocolate and nuts.

3 Drop large teaspoons of the mixture on to greased baking trays and bake for 15 minutes. Leave to cool for about 1 minute before transferring to a wire rack.

CHOCOLATE CAKE

MAKES ONE 20CM (8IN) ROUND CAKE

FOR THE CAKE
6 medium eggs, separated • 175g (6oz) caster sugar
250g (8oz) plain chocolate, melted • 30g (1oz) cornflour
15g (½oz) cocoa powder

TO COMPLETE
160g (5½oz) plain chocolate • 100ml (3½fl oz) crème fraîche

1 Preheat the oven to 180°C/350°F/Gas 4. Grease a deep 20cm (8in) round cake tin and line the base with greaseproof paper. Whisk the egg yolks and 90g (3oz) of the sugar until pale and thick. Fold in the melted chocolate.

2 Whisk the egg whites until stiff, gradually adding the remaining sugar. Fold the egg whites into the chocolate mixture using a large metal spoon. Sift together the cornflour and cocoa powder and fold into the mixture. Spoon into the prepared tin and bake for 35 minutes or until risen. Leave in the tin for 5 minutes before turning out on to a wire rack to cool completely.

3 Melt 100g (3½oz) of the chocolate and stir in the crème fraîche. Swirl over the cooled cake. Using a vegetable peeler, make curls from the remaining chocolate and sprinkle on top of the cake. Tie a ribbon around the cake.

LUXURY FRUIT CAKE

MAKES ONE 23CM (9IN) ROUND CAKE

100ml (3½fl oz) dark rum • 100ml (3½fl oz) medium-dry sherry
90ml (3fl oz) water • 1kg (2lb) luxury dried mixed fruits
2tbsp ground mixed spice • 1tbsp unrefined molasses sugar
225g (7½oz) butter • 350g (11½oz) soft light-brown sugar
5 medium eggs, beaten • 225g (7½oz) self-raising flour
100g (3½oz) mixed nuts, chopped

TO COMPLETE
4tbsp sieved apricot jam, warmed • 1kg (2lb) white marzipan
1tbsp vodka or gin • 1kg (2lb) ready-to-roll icing or 1kg (2lb) royal
icing mix (made according to packet instructions)

1 Pour the rum, sherry and water into a pan and stir in the dried mixed fruit, mixed spice and molasses sugar. Bring to the boil, then simmer for 15 minutes, stirring occasionally. Leave to cool.

2 Preheat the oven to 160°C/325°F/Gas 3, then grease and line a deep 23cm (9in) round cake tin. Cream the butter and sugar until pale and light, then gradually beat in the eggs. Sift the flour and fold it into the cake mixture using a large metal spoon. Stir in the nuts, then the cooled fruit mixture and liquid.

3 Spoon the mixture into the prepared cake tin. Level the surface and make a shallow well in the centre to ensure a level top once cooked. Bake for 3 hours or until a skewer inserted into the centre comes out clean. Leave to cool in the tin. Remove the lining paper and wrap in fresh greaseproof paper and foil. Store in a cool, dry place for up to one month. The cake can be iced up to two weeks before serving.

4 To marzipan the cake, first brush it with the warmed apricot jam. Roll the marzipan into a round large enough to cover the top and sides of the cake. Once in position, smooth the marzipan using your hands or an icing smoother. Leave to dry for at least 1 hour.

5 Brush the marzipan with the vodka or gin. Roll the ready-to-roll icing into a round large enough to cover the top and sides of the cake. Carefully position it over the cake and smooth. If using royal icing, spread on to the cake and smooth or make peaks using a fork.

Madeira Cake

THE VARIATIONS THAT FOLLOW THIS CAKE RECIPE MAKE
IT PERFECT FOR SPECIAL OCCASIONS.

300g (10oz) unsalted butter • 300g (10oz) golden caster sugar
6 medium eggs, beaten • 175g (6oz) self-raising flour
175g (6oz) plain flour • 90g (3oz) ground almonds
grated zest and juice of 2 medium oranges

1 Preheat the oven to 180°C/350°F/Gas 4. Butter and
line a deep 23cm (9in) round cake tin.

2 Cream the butter and sugar until pale and light.
Gradually beat in the eggs, adding a little sifted flour
to prevent the mixture curdling.

3 Sift the remaining flours together and add the
almonds. Fold the flour and almond mixture into
the creamed mixture with the orange zest and juice.

4 Spoon into the prepared tin and bake for 35 minutes.
Reduce the temperature to 160°C/325°F/Gas 3 and cook
for a further 45 minutes or until a skewer inserted in the
centre comes out clean. Turn out on to a wire rack to cool.

Teddy Bear

1 Cut the cake into a teddy-bear shape and use the
trimmings to make a slightly raised tummy and cheeks.
Brush the cake with a little warmed sieved apricot jam.

2 Knead 1kg (2lb) of ready-to-roll icing with 30g (1oz)
sifted cocoa powder. When evenly coloured, roll out
the icing and use to cover the cake, gently pressing the
sides to emphasize the bear shape. Mark lines on the
paws. Use a little white and black icing, tinted with food
colouring, to make eyes, a nose and a mouth.

Ladybird

1 Cut the cake into a dome-shaped body and use the
trimmings to make a small head. Brush the cake with
a little warmed sieved apricot jam.

2 Colour 500g (1lb) of ready-to-roll icing red and 125g
(4oz) black, and roll both thinly. Use the red icing to
cover the body and the black icing to make spots. Use
black trimmings to make small antennae and leave to set
for about 30 minutes before attaching them to the head.

Champagne Bottle

1 Trim the cake to a fat champagne bottle shape and
brush with a little warmed sieved apricot jam.

2 Roll 625g (1¼lb) of white marzipan thinly and use to
cover the cake. Leave for at least 1 hour. Knead 625g
(1¼lb) of ready-to-roll icing and colour it dark green with
food colouring; when evenly coloured, roll out and use to
cover the cake. Roll 60g (2oz) of white icing, cut to a label
shape and pipe on the recipient's name or the occasion.

3 To make champagne truffles, stir together 125g (4oz)
melted white chocolate, 3 tablespoons double cream,
3 tablespoons champagne and 60g (2oz) cake crumbs. Chill
until firm. Shape into 25 balls, dip in 175g (6oz) melted
white chocolate and leave to set. Arrange around the cake.

Wedding Cake

1 Double the cake ingredients. Put one-third of the
mixture in a prepared 15cm (6in) deep cake tin and
two-thirds in a 23cm (9in) tin. Bake for 40 minutes before
turning the oven temperature down. Cook the small cake
for a further 25 minutes, the larger one for 45 minutes.

2 Cover the cakes with 375g (12oz) of orange-flavoured
buttercream. Roll 750g (1½lb) of white ready-to-roll
icing thinly and use to cover the larger cake. Roll another
375g (12oz) of icing and use to cover the smaller cake.

3 Place the small cake on top of the large cake, then
pipe a fine trail of royal icing around the base of
each. Decorate the cake with a garland of fresh flowers.

Christening Cake

1 Make the cake mixture as instructed and spoon into
a buttered and lined 23cm (9in) petal-shaped tin. Bake
for 40 minutes, then reduce the oven temperature and
bake for a further 55 minutes. Leave to cool.

2 Brush the cake with warmed sieved apricot jam. Roll
750g (1½lb) of white marzipan and use to cover the
cake. Leave for 1 hour. Knead 1.25kg (2½lb) of ready-to-roll
icing and colour, if wished. Roll and use to cover the cake.

3 Pipe the child's name on the cake using a little royal
icing; pipe a little more icing around the base of the
cake, if wished. Decorate with flowers cut from 60g (2oz)
ready-to-roll icing, coloured as desired.

LARGE PARTIES, BALLS AND WEDDINGS CAN NEVER BE

PLANNED TOO SOON. THE SECRET OF SUCCESS IS TO TAKE A

YEAR TO ORGANIZE A TRADITIONAL WEDDING, AND UP TO SIX MONTHS

FOR A LARGE-SCALE PARTY: WRITE A TIME PLAN AND STICK TO IT.

BOOK A VENUE EARLY – IF YOU FIND A BETTER PLACE, YOU CAN ALWAYS

PLANNING
A PARTY

CANCEL A PROVISIONAL BOOKING. COLLECT INSPIRATIONAL PICTURES,

MENUS AND PRICE LISTS, AND ASK FRIENDS FOR RECOMMENDATIONS ON

MUSIC AND FOOD. SAMPLE FOOD BEFORE A BOOKING. LISTEN,

EITHER LIVE OR ON TAPE, TO THE MUSIC OR ENTERTAINMENT,

AND GIVE A PLAY-LIST WELL IN ADVANCE. ABOVE ALL DELEGATE,

ASKING FRIENDS AND FAMILY TO HELP MAKE THE DAY UNFORGETTABLE.

ESSENTIALS

TO ENSURE GREAT SUCCESS FOR A

SPECIAL PARTY, GIVE THOUGHT TO

THESE BASICS BEFORE ALL ELSE.

WHEN & WHERE

Make the timing and setting of the party your earliest decision. Exact dates and venues can be inked in later, but decide now roughly on the time of year and kind of venue you would prefer. To increase party space at home, consider using a specialist firm to erect a marquee.

BUDGET

How much you want or can afford to spend should be set firmly at the outset, and the amount adhered to. For some, food may be more important than drinks. Others may want to spend more on entertainment or the venue. Whatever your choice, bear in mind that a drinks party is usually less expensive than a seated meal for a large number of people, especially if the meal involves hiring equipment and paying professional staff to help. Borrowing tables, chairs, linen and tableware rather than hiring them gives a big saving. Budget is a major factor in menu-planning, determining what you can or cannot serve (*see opposite*).

THEME & DECOR

See pages 8–73 for a myriad party theme ideas. Decide on the size of your budget, then adapt the idea to suit the occasion. Pay special attention to lighting – it can transform a dingy venue. On a big budget, seek the help of florists and interior designers to bring originality and drama to a party.

GUEST LIST & NUMBERS

The length of the guest list will be dictated by the type of event you are planning and the size of your budget. Plan the list early and be flexible, allowing for a few late invitations.

★ **Ideal numbers for parties:** small party, up to 30 guests; medium party, 30–100 guests; large party, over 100.

ENTERTAINMENT

Entertainment choices are listed on page 122. To avoid disappointment, watch the entertainment live prior to booking or listen to a sample tape. Give a band or DJ a play-list in advance to ensure guests enjoy the music. Remember that entertainers will need a private dressing-room at the venue.

FOOD & DRINK

If you are planning to use a catering company, ask friends for recommendations and consider how you would like the food and drink to be served. Options include:

★ **Stand-up fork buffets** allow good interaction between guests, who can circulate freely. Generally cheaper than full sit-down meals, they allow for a greater choice of food, with lots of different dishes.

★ **Seated fork buffets** allow a cold starter to be pre-set at the table. Some guests prefer to sit while eating.

★ **Sit-down meals** are best for formal occasions. Table-planning ensures that like-minded guests can be seated next to each other. More expensive than fork buffets, a sit-down meal should include at least three courses.

★ **Cocktail parties** (*see pages 8–13*) are ideal for entertaining large numbers, when it is an advantage that not everyone arrives at once and that some guests only stay half an hour. Cocktail parties generally last 2½ hours.

★ **Drinks,** both alcoholic and non-alcoholic, should be plentiful. When assessing suppliers, which may include off-licences, wine merchants and supermarkets, ask if they provide on a sale-or-return basis and if they deliver and supply glasses.

VENUE IDEAS

There are exciting party venue ideas on page 49, and a list of wedding venues on page 34. Here are more ideas to inspire:

★ **Leisure and cultural:** theatre, cinema, museum, amusement arcade, burger bar, wine bar or cellar, health club.

★ **Indoor sporting:** sports club, swimming pool, bowling alley, cricket pavilion, boat club, ice-skating rink.

★ **Outdoors:** theme park, narrow boat or river cruiser, activity centre, log cabin, lake, public gardens.

★ **With a difference:** double-decker bus, steam train, pier, ferry, hot-air balloon, fairground, barn, ski piste.

PLANNING 2

THE BIG MATTERS DECIDED, MORE DETAILED PLANNING CAN NOW BEGIN.

INVITATIONS

Send out invitations at least two months before a large event to allow guests time to make travel plans and arrangements. A reply card, with a reply-by-date, helps guests. Ensure that you state the dress code for the party on the invitation.

MENU

When planning the menu, as well as budgetary factors, consider who is coming; whether guests are young or old; any specific dietary requirements, such as vegetarian, vegan, halal, kosher; whether a special occasion demands specific food. Sample a menu if you are using outside caterers before confirming the booking.

★ **Plan a good range** of tastes and textures. Include a varied mix of ingredients, trying not to repeat them in different dishes, and think of colour and presentation, course by course. Try not to overload a meal with calories and never be too sparing with portions.

★ **Food at drinks parties** should be bite-sized for ease of eating. Always provide cocktail napkins. Allow 10 pieces per head for a cocktail party of approximately two hours; for longer durations, allow 15-20 pieces per head.

DRINKS & GLASSES

Drinks should be ready to offer as guests arrive. It is disastrous for a party to run dry, so order drinks generously on a sale-or-return basis. Remember that unused bottles must be returned completely intact, including labels.

★ **Allow 3–4 glasses per guest.** Guests served from trays will put a glass back on the tray and take another one.

★ **Provide plenty of chilled mineral water** and soft drinks, especially in hot weather. One bottle of mineral water serves approximately 5 glasses.

★ **One bottle of wine** serves 5-6 glasses. Allow two-thirds of a bottle of white wine and one-third of red wine per guest. If only wine or champagne is being served, allow half a bottle per guest.

BUFFETS

Set buffet tables at each end of the room so guests don't all have to queue in one place. Use tables large enough to allow space for plates, cutlery, napkins and condiments as well as the food. Avoid bottlenecks by setting buffet tables well away from a bar. To prevent queuing, invite small groups of people up to the table in turn to fetch their food.

SEATING PLAN

A seating plan should combine an alphabetical list of guests and their table numbers with a numbered table plan, both positioned at the entrance to the dining area. Give someone a copy of the list to help those who cannot find their table. At a sit-down meal, choose round tables for 8, 10 or 12 guests.

★ **Have a contingency plan** for "no shows", so that if a guest at the main table does not arrive, the place can be filled by another guest.

★ **Use place setting cards** at formal, sit-down occasions. It is useful to have the name on both sides of the card so that guests know who is sitting opposite them.

STAFF

While you may be able to cope well using volunteers at a party at home, at an outside venue, it is best to employ professional staff. Allow one waiter per 20 guests at a drinks party, and one per 10 at a sit-down meal. Depending on the event and venue, you will need bar, reception, cloakroom and security staff, and car-park attendants. Disco organizers and bands are responsible for bringing and setting up their own equipment. At home, keep the kitchen separate from the party room so that sounds of clearing up are not heard.

VENUE

Use the checklists on pages 122–23 to ensure that your chosen venue and its decoration are perfect on the day.

SCHEDULE

A schedule helps everyone know who is doing what and at what time. At home, make sure neighbours know of plans for a party well in advance.

Checklists 3

WORK YOUR WAY THROUGH THE

FOLLOWING LISTS, TICKING OFF

ITEMS AS YOU DEAL WITH THEM;

THEY WILL HELP ENSURE THAT ANY

PARTY, LARGE OR SMALL, GOES

WITHOUT A HITCH AND BECOMES

AN EVENT THAT GUESTS WILL

ALWAYS REMEMBER.

Food & Drink

DEPENDING ON THE NATURE OF YOUR PARTY, USE THIS LIST TO ENSURE THAT YOU HAVE THE ESSENTIALS FOR SERVING THE FOOD AND DRINK YOU HAVE SELECTED.

★ Sufficient tables and chairs, including buffet table, gift table, cake table, occasional tables, babies' high chairs. ❑
★ Table linen, napkins. ❑
★ China, including for tea, coffee. ❑
★ Cutlery, for three-course meals, tea, coffee. ❑
★ Condiments for savoury and sweet dishes, tea, coffee. ❑
★ Serving dishes, bowls, cake knife and utensils. ❑
★ Serving dishes/stands for special foods, e.g. cakes. ❑
★ Adequate cooking, food-warming facilities. ❑
★ Glasses for alcoholic and soft drinks. ❑
★ Ice, ice bucket and tongs. ❑
★ Cocktail shaker, stirrers and twizzle sticks. ❑
★ Bottle openers and corkscrews. ❑
★ Serving trays and napkins. ❑
★ Fruit for decorating drinks with, knife, board. ❑
★ Refrigerator within reach of bar/serving table. ❑
★ Seating plan at entrance, if necessary. ❑

Venue

FOR A VENUE OTHER THAN YOUR OWN HOME, USE THIS LIST IN ADVANCE TO CHECK THE SUITABILITY OF THE SPACE FOR THE PARTY YOU ARE PLANNING.

★ Number of guests the reception rooms hold. ❑
★ Availability and quality of cloakrooms, toilets. ❑
★ Lighting, ventilation, heating of reception rooms. ❑
★ Availability of cutlery, china, table linen, etc. ❑
★ Standard of catering, menus, if available. ❑
★ Use of outside caterers, florists, entertainers. ❑
★ Adequate kitchen facilities for outside caterers. ❑
★ Presence of administrative staff for advice, liaison. ❑
★ PA system for speeches. ❑
★ Possibility of bringing one's own decorations. ❑
★ Easy to reach by car or public transport. ❑
★ Closeness, ease of car parking. ❑
★ Facilities for disabled, including entrance ramps. ❑
★ State of fire alarms, emergency exits, security. ❑
★ Any other events at the venue on your date. ❑

Entertainment

CONSIDER THESE AS POSSIBILITIES FOR MAKING YOUR PARTY MEMORABLE, CHOOSING ENTERTAINMENT TO COMPLEMENT AND ENHANCE THE EVENT.

★ Disco and DJ. ❑
★ Dance floor: hire if the venue's is inadequate. ❑
★ Live band/orchestra/string quartet. ❑
★ Master of Ceremonies (MC). ❑
★ Entertainers for adult parties: singer, comedian. ❑
★ Entertainers for children's parties: magician, puppeteer. ❑
★ Informal entertainers, such as stilt-walkers, fire-eaters, magicians, jugglers, etc., moving among guests. ❑
★ Firework display. ❑
★ Laser show. ❑
★ Casino. ❑
★ Quiz night, with compere. ❑
★ Barn- or line-dance caller and musicians. ❑
★ Funfair attractions. ❑
★ Indoor sports competitions, e.g. darts, boules. ❑

DECORATION

USE DECORATIONS TO SET THE MOOD FOR A PARTY, ENHANCING THE THEME OF THE OCCASION AND MAKING THE VENUE LOOK WELCOMING AND FUN.

★ Table arrangements, low table centrepieces. ❑

★ Decorative napkins, place settings for tables. ❑

★ Place setting cards. ❑

★ Flowers, large-scale floral decorations. ❑

★ Lighting: candles, scented candles, tapers, night-lights, incense, lamps, fairy lights. ❑

★ Balloons (and means to inflate them), streamers, string spray, party poppers, disposable cameras, crackers. ❑

★ Entrance decoration. ❑

★ Chair decorations. ❑

★ Decorative party bags for children. ❑

★ Favours and gifts. ❑

★ Banners, paper lanterns. ❑

★ Weights to tie helium-filled balloons to. ❑

EQUIPMENT

HIRING EQUIPMENT FOR A PARTY MAY RELIEVE YOU OF ORGANIZATIONAL PROBLEMS AND EXPENSE, BUT MANY RESPONSIBILITIES REMAIN.

★ Equipment delivered in good time before the event, so that it can be checked, wrong items returned and missing items replaced. ❑

★ Glassware, china, etc. checked as soon as received; suppliers informed of any breakages. ❑

★ Discos/live bands have enough time to set up equipment and sound check – allow two hours before the party starts. ❑

★ Tent- or marquee-hire company has enough time to erect tent, assemble equipment and remove it afterwards (check with specialist company). ❑

★ Dance floor assembled, if necessary. ❑

★ PA system for speeches in place. ❑

★ Entertainers have all equipment/space needed. ❑

★ Entertainment such as firework or laser display, casino, fun fair or sports equipment installed and double-checked. ❑

STAFF & CLEARING UP

WHETHER YOU USE PAID PROFESSIONALS OR VOLUNTEERS FROM THE FAMILY, KEEP IN MIND THESE KEY CONSIDERATIONS TO CHECK ON THE DAY.

★ Staff are well turned out. ❑

★ Administrative and catering staff have schedule and timings for the day. ❑

★ Waiters are briefed on the food and drink served. ❑

★ Waiters know which guests need special attention or have special food requirements. ❑

★ Bar staff, reception and cloakroom staff, security staff and carpark attendants are in place. ❑

★ At home, you have help to prepare food, wash up and clear up afterwards. ❑

★ Every home helper has a specific task and is thoroughly briefed. ❑

★ Clearing-up essentials are to hand: rubbish sacks, brushes, mop, vacuum cleaner, detergent, rubber gloves, tea towels, air freshener, dustbins. ❑

EXTRAS

OUTSIDE IMMEDIATE PARTY CONCERNS, A CARING HOST SHOULD PAY ATTENTION TO EXTRA DETAILS TO MAKE ANY OCCASION REALLY SPECIAL.

★ Road maps, bus and train timetables sent out with invitations. ❑

★ Availability of taxis from and back to station/bus depots checked. ❑

★ Private transport arranged, if necessary (tell guests in advance if they are expected to pay for it). ❑

★ Accommodation for out-of-town guests checked. List (with prices) of local hotels, motels, etc. sent with invitations. ❑

★ Home or venue insurance, includes cover for theft of gifts, loss of jewellery, damage to cars in carpark, accidents to guests, etc. ❑

★ Well-equipped first-aid kit, with telephone numbers for doctor and ambulance. ❑

★ Soap, hand towels and sewing kits in bathrooms. ❑

★ Parting gifts for guests, party bags for children. ❑

COUNTDOWN 4

THIS PLAN ALLOWS SIX MONTHS

TO ARRANGE THE PERFECT PARTY. YOU

MAY NOT NEED THIS MUCH TIME, SO

ADAPT THE COUNTDOWN TO SUIT

YOUR REQUIREMENTS.

MONTH 6

★ Choose party theme. ❑
★ Decide on guest numbers. ❑
★ Plan type of entertainment. ❑
★ Decide how much money to spend. ❑
★ Research and short-list suitable venues/caterers. ❑
★ Visit short-listed venues/caterers. ❑
★ Discuss with venues/caterers what is included in their charges, outlining any extras you may need and confirming that they can supply them. ❑
★ Research entertainment and ask for examples of work e.g. video/tape recordings, or go to see live. ❑
★ Check estimates off against budget. ❑

MONTH 5

★ Make final choice of venue/caterer, confirming the date and requesting detailed contract(s). ❑
★ Make final choice of entertainment. ❑
★ If you want a photographer, research suitable ones. ❑
★ Pay deposits. ❑

MONTH 4

★ Prepare wording for all printed material, e.g. invitations, menus, place setting cards, programmes. Research and select a printer. ❑
★ Make final choice of photographer and confirm date. ❑
★ Organize and book transport. ❑
★ Hold initial planning meeting with venue/caterer. ❑
★ Plan a complete programme of the work needed between now and the party date. ❑

MONTH 3

★ Check proofs of all printed material and collect final copy from the printer. ❑
★ Mail invitations (plus map, hotel list, etc.), requesting replies and notes of dietary needs. Monitor replies. ❑
★ Select and buy gifts. ❑
★ Sample and confirm menu choice and other catering requirements with venue/caterers. ❑
★ Check estimates against budget; are you on course? ❑

MONTH 2

★ Draw up seating plan. ❑
★ Plan flowers and floral decorations; book florists. ❑
★ Hold update meetings with venue/caterer, entertainers, using the checklists on pages 122-23 as necessary. ❑

MONTH 1

★ Send final guest list to venue/caterer, with confirmation of menu and dietary requirements. ❑
★ Use a final meeting with venue/caterer to check all arrangements. ❑
★ Process invoices requiring payment before the party. ❑
★ Draw up a schedule and timing for the day. ❑

THE BIG DAY

★ On arrival, check that the venue is clean and tidy and that toilets and cloakrooms are clean. ❑
★ Check the venue for damage before equipment arrives. ❑
★ Check that all hired equipment is on site, that printed matter has been delivered and that gifts are present. ❑
★ Reconfirm catering numbers to venue/caterer, and provide final table/seating plan, plus place setting cards. ❑
★ Put up decorations and put out gifts. ❑
★ Ensure venue/caterer and entertainers have your final party timings and schedule. ❑
★ Maintain constant touch with venue/caterer and entertainers throughout the party. ❑

THE DAY AFTER

★ Ensure all equipment is returned to suppliers, checking that no damage has been done to it or to the venue. ❑
★ Check all invoices in detail before payment. ❑
★ Write thank you letters to suppliers. ❑
★ Start planning your next party! ❑

HINTS & TIPS

5

BOTH HOSTS AND GUESTS HAVE

LARGE PARTS TO PLAY IN A PARTY'S

SUCCESS. FOLLOW THESE TIPS,

AND EVERYONE WILL HAVE

A GREAT TIME.

TIPS FOR HOSTS

★ Ensure that guests are each given a drink on arrival, or have ready a bowl of punch and glasses for guests to help themselves to.

★ Be a vigilant host and make an effort to introduce guests to people with whom they have something in common.

★ Keep guests mingling. Ask male guests to move on two places at the end of each course at a dinner party; make the ladies ask the men to dance every fifth dance; keep the party confined to two or three rooms so guests can't spread out far.

★ Make sure that a professional photographer does not interrupt the flow of the party and uses his camera discreetly; formally posed photographs involving numbers of guests, as at a wedding, should be taken before the event or reception is well underway.

ETIQUETTE FOR GUESTS

★ When invited to a party, reply as soon as possible; if you cannot attend, thank your host for the invitation.

★ Be considerate: do not arrive at the party with more guests than the host has invited. If your children are not named on the invite, they probably are not expected.

★ Be punctual: lateness is no longer as fashionable as it used to be.

★ Dress according to the time of day and the type of occasion, observing any dress code on the invitation.

★ If you bring a still or video camera to the party, use it discreetly to avoid bringing the party to a halt.

★ Be a good guest: wear the name badge or funny hat the host hands out, and take part enthusiastically in ice-breaking games or competitions.

★ If you wish to smoke, be considerate of others: ask your host or other guests at the table before lighting up, and never stub out cigarettes in the table china or glasses. If in doubt, smoke outside.

★ If, at the last minute, something happens to prevent you attending the party, try your best to notify the host.

COPING WITH HANGOVERS

Having a hangover is often part and parcel of a party, but it does not have to be. There are a few good ways to avoid a hangover and several methods of getting rid of one.

★ Have a good meal before going to a party: food slows down alcohol absorption. If you have no time to eat, at least drink milk.

★ Avoid mixing grape and grain (wine and beer); stick to one type and brand of drink throughout a party.

★ Go easy on smoking: it makes you want to drink more.

★ Make every third or fourth drink a soft drink, top up wine with soda or sparkling mineral water to make spritzers, and drink spirits with mixers.

★ Know your limit and be ready to say "no thanks". Don't be egged on to "have one for the road".

If, once the party is over, you know you have drunk more than you should, there are ways to minimize the effects:

★ Walk home, if possible. The exercise and the fresh air will make you feel better.

★ Drink a pint of cold water and go to the lavatory before going to bed. The water helps rehydrate the body.

★ The next morning, drink fresh orange and citrus fruit juices and have a good breakfast.

★ Go for a walk, swim or jog the next day, or enjoy a leisurely sauna and massage.

★ If all else fails, and drastic measures are called for the next day, take the hair of the dog – mix yourself a Bloody Mary to help settle your stomach.

INDEX

Page numbers for party themes are in **bold**; those for recipes are in *italics*.

ACKNOWLEDGMENTS

Lauren Floodgate's Acknowledgments
I am indebted above all to my husband, Richard, thank you for your tireless support behind the scenes; to my mum, Hazel Floodgate, I couldn't have done it without you – enthusiastic, patient and brimming with good ideas and, yes, you can type faster and more accurately than me! My sister, Bryony Hoad, who has such good taste and worked so hard designing and making all the beautiful projects; Simon Smith, the consummate professional and a very good friend, thank you for your recommendation, I hope I did you justice; Simon's assistant Alex MacDonald, who kept us going with

intravenous coffee and tales of his exploits; Lucy and Sarah for the delicious recipes and wonderful food; Clare Hunt for her support and thoughtful styling; and to all my friends who so kindly shared their ideas.

A special thanks to my designer, Tracey Ward, and my editor, Monica Chakraverty, two more patient, hard-working and agreeable colleagues I couldn't have wished for; and to Susannah Marriott and Carole Ash, who invited me to write the book.
Final thanks to Mary-Jane Vaughan at Fast Flowers, 609 Fulham Road, Fulham, London, SW6 5UA (0171 381 6422), for supplying the

stunning flowers and arrangements, and to Penny Harrison at Homecrafts Direct (0116 251 3139), for supplying all the craft materials used in the projects.

Publisher's Acknowledgements
Dorling Kindersley would like to thank Janice Anderson for editorial help; Sue Bosanko for the index; Brightside; Emy Manby and Rachana Shah for design assistance; Dorothy Ward for help with props. Additional photography by: Peter Chadwick, Philip Dowell, Steve Gorton, Stephen Hayward, Dave King, Ian O'Leary, Stephen Oliver, Tim Ridley and Stephen Schott.